The Future of Data Platforms: Cloud Databases and Big Data Technologies

Manoj Kumar

Purushotham Jinka

Prakash Parida

Shyam Goyal

notionpress.com

INDIA • SINGAPORE • MALAYSIA

ISBN

Paperback 979-8-90451-137-1

Hardcase 979-8-90451-138-8

Preface

In the era of digital transformation, data platforms have become central to innovation, scalability, and intelligent decision-making. The emergence of cloud databases and big data technologies has significantly reshaped the way organizations store, process, and analyze information.

This book, The Future of Data Platforms: Cloud Databases and Big Data Technologies, presents a concise yet meaningful exploration of the evolving landscape of modern data systems. It is intended to provide students, researchers, academicians, and professionals with a structured understanding of cloud-native architectures, distributed data processing, and emerging trends in data engineering.

We hope this work serves as a valuable academic and professional reference for readers seeking insight into the future of data-driven technologies.

Dedication

This book is dedicated to all learners, researchers, engineers, and technology enthusiasts who believe in the transformative power of data.

We dedicate this work to the innovators and problem-solvers who continue to push the boundaries of what is possible through cloud computing, big data, and intelligent digital systems. Your curiosity, persistence, and vision inspire the advancement of knowledge and technology.

We also dedicate this book to our families, mentors, colleagues, and well-wishers whose encouragement, patience, and support have been invaluable throughout this journey. Their belief in our efforts has been a constant source of motivation.

Finally, this work is dedicated to the future generation of data professionals and scholars who will shape the next era of digital transformation with creativity, responsibility, and purpose.

ACKNOWLEDGEMENT

The authors wish to express their sincere gratitude to all those who have contributed, directly or indirectly, to the completion of this book.

We are deeply thankful to our families for their constant encouragement, patience, and understanding throughout the writing process. Their unwavering support has been a source of strength and motivation.

We also extend our heartfelt appreciation to our teachers, mentors, academic guides, and professional colleagues whose knowledge, guidance, and valuable insights have significantly enriched this work. Their encouragement and intellectual support have played an important role in shaping the ideas presented in this book.

The authors further acknowledge the wider academic and professional communities whose contributions in cloud computing, database systems, distributed architectures, and big data technologies have provided a strong foundation for this publication.

Finally, we express our sincere thanks to all readers, students, professionals, and institutions whose support and inspiration made this scholarly effort possible. It is our hope that this book will serve as a meaningful academic and professional resource.

Contents

CHAPTER 1

EVOLUTION OF DATA PLATFORMS

1.1 TRADITIONAL DATABASES AND DATA WAREHOUSES

During the first phase of the digital transformation, organizations depended so much on the conventional database systems to store and handle the operational data of the organizations. These systems were mainly used to support the transactional systems like banking systems, "enterprise resource planning" (ERP), customer relationship management and inventory management. The traditional databases focused on structured data storage, consistency and reliability, which guaranteed that business transactions would be carried out efficiently and accurately. Relational database management systems (RDBMS) emerged as the primary method of managing the enterprise data over the years due to their high data integrity and standard query functions.

The need to have systems that could be employed to undertake analytical processing also became more significant as organizations kept on producing higher levels of data. Although the traditional databases proved to be very advantageous in regard to the day to day running of an organization, it was not suitable in the complex analytical queries that involved large volumes of data. In order to deal with this issue, the idea of data warehouses was developed. The data warehouses were developed to gather, combine, and save data among various systems of operation in a single centralized repository that would allow organizations conduct extensive analysis and produce strategic information.

Data warehouses brought about a systematic way of decision support systems by arranging the past data in a format that is used in reporting and analysis. They enabled business to engage in complicated queries, create business intelligence reports, and uncover tendencies in business information. Data warehouses also facilitated the use of data to make decisions by enabling separation of analytical workloads off operational databases in addition to improving performance of the systems.

Even though traditional databases and data warehouses were good, there were several limitations to them as data volumes were increasing, data variety and processing requirements and demands were mounting. The systems frequently were built on infrastructures and hardened scheme, which were not responsive to the dynamically evolving data environments. The need to ensure more scalable and flexible data platforms was realized with the advent of modern data architectures with the onset of using cloud computing and big data technology by organizations.

1.1.1 Relational Database Management Systems (RDBMS)

Computer software used to store, modify, and query structured data based on a relational model is called a relational database management system (RDBMS). This model's data is organised into tables, sometimes referred to as relations, with rows and columns. Tables show specific entities (users, orders, etc.), and keys—primary keys, which are unique row IDs, and foreign keys, which are pointers to other rows in separate tables—are used to construct associations between entities. SQL (Structured Query Language), which allows a developer to create, read, update, and remove data as well as enforce constraints such data types and relationships, is the standard language used to interface with an RDBMS. Popular RDBMS include Microsoft SQL Server, PostgreSQL, and MySQL.

One of the main properties of RDBMS is that, it will implement data integrity using ACID (Atomicity, Consistency, isolation, Durability) properties. As an example, atomicity means that a series of operations (transactions) is either completed or the entire process is rolled back in their entirety without a half-complete change. Consistency ensures that the data is valid as per the set of rules (e.g. the email of a user must be unique). Isolation also means that concurrent transactions do not interfere with one another and durability is used to ensure that the data withstands the system failure. The following properties render RDBMS an appropriate choice when it is necessary to have reliable transactions in the application, e.g. banking system or inventory management. Also, RDBMS facilitates complex queries like joins that are used to combine data of various tables based on the relationship that allow the effective analysis of related data.

RDBMS would best fit in applications where data relationships and consistency are very important. Considering an example of an e-commerce platform, customers, orders and products may be represented in tables, where orders and customers are connected by a foreign key and orders and products by a foreign key. Although alternative databases like the NoSQL databases are good at unstructured data, or performing horizontally, RDBMS is still the database of choice when it comes to structured data that is required to have a schema. The cooperation of developers with such tools as the JSONB type of PostgreSQL or stored procedures of MySQL is often used to add functionality and ensure relational integrity. Knowledge of the fundamentals of RDBMS: tables, keys, SQL, and ACID are useful in enabling developers to design systems that facilitate the balancing of flexibility, reliability, and performance.

RDBMS traditional platforms had been at the core of the enterprise data management over a number of decades. Relational databases have been widely used in organizations to store the business applications of an organization as banking system, inventory management, customer relationship management and enterprise resource planning as the enterprise computing grew in the 1980s and 1990s. These systems have offered a credible means of controlling structured business data besides guaranteeing accuracy and uniformity in transactions. With the growth of the enterprise information systems, the relational databases were the backbone of several organizational data infrastructures. Nevertheless, as digital data, both semi-structured and unstructured, grew fast, the systems based on the conventional RDBMS started to have certain problems with scalability and flexibility. These constraints later promoted the introduction of new data management systems, such as data warehouses, distributed databases, and emerging big data systems.

1.1.2 Architecture and Working of Data Warehouses

Data warehouse architecture refers to a design outline or framework that defines the arrangement of data storage, management, access and organization of data in a data warehouse system (DWH). It establishes the movement of data among various working systems to a central database where it could be counted and analysed. Conversing raw data into valuable insights consists of a number of components, processes and interactions that collaborate in the architecture. In this organized architecture, organizations can combine information in various sources and make it ready to be analysed.

An effective data warehouse architecture can assist organizations to effectively manage big and complicated datasets. The architecture allows uniting the data of various operational systems to a single repository, which is used to serve reporting, business intelligence, and analytical applications. Data warehouses are created to handle analytical workloads more as opposed to transactional workloads which enable organizations to analyses historical and integrated data to aid the decision-making process.

Data warehouse architecture also establishes a single source of truth of an organization since information of different systems is brought together to a single environment. The same underlying data can be accessed by different stakeholders but the type of analysis is done varies based on the needs of the different stakeholders. This enables business analysts, managers and technical teams to have common data but use various analytical models and reporting techniques.

Data Warehouse Layers:

In data warehousing the structure is usually layered in order to simplify the processing and analysis of the data. All the layers fulfil certain functions that equip data to be used in analytics.

- **Source Layer:** The source layer is a layer which involves the origin of data, which is built on various databases and working systems. The data can be defined as relational databases, NoSQL databases, APIs, enterprise applications or other systems of operations. The main data that is stored in this layer are raw operational data that will be extracted in the future to be processed.
- **Staging Layer:** The staging layer is a temporary layer that gathers the data that would be eventually loaded into the data warehouse. Here, data is purified, verified and processed using ETL (Extract, Transform, Load) or ELT (Extract, Load, Transform) operations.

The staging area serves as a processing intermediary area where raw data is ready to be integrated and used in an analytical manner.

- **Modelling Layer:** Within the modelling layer structured data is shaped into formats enabling them to be used in analytic querying and reporting. Data is organized with the help of data models like star schema or snowflake schema. These models store data in fact tables and dimension tables in order to enable analytical systems to effectively use complex queries.
- **Presentation Layer:** The presentation layer or consumption layer is a layer that offers access and utilization tools to the user to access and analyze the data stored. The visualization tools, reporting, dashboards, and business intelligence platforms enable users to engage with the data warehouse and create analytical information.

Core Components of Data Warehouse Architecture:

An architecture of a data warehouse is a structure of a number of interrelated components that collaborate with each other to converting raw data of operation into valuable analytical data.

- **Data Warehouse Database**: Data warehouse is the central part of the warehouse and is where the integrated data is stored in a form that is efficient in analysis and reporting. The database can be adopted based on relational database systems, analytical databases, cloud-based databases, or a specialized data warehouse platform based on the requirements of the organization.
- **Data Integration:** Data integration consists of the processes of combining and getting the information ready of different sources so that it can be analysed efficiently. The typical forms of integration are ETL and ELT processes which retrieve data out of the source systems, convert it to the suitable formats and insert it into the data warehouse. These procedures make sure that information becomes consistent, correct and that it is analytical ready.
- **Metadata:** Metadata is information regarding the information stored in the warehouse. It contains information concerning information sources, structure, transformations, and connections among information sets. Metadata assists the users and systems to comprehend the meaning, origin and utilization of the information in the warehouse.

- **Data Warehouse Access Tools:** This is a data warehouse system that needs tools through which the stored information can be accessed and analysed by the user. These tools are query and reporting tools, Online Analytical Processing (OLAP) systems, data mining tools, and business intelligence platforms, which aid in exploring and analysing of data by users.

Types of Data Warehouse Architecture:

Organizations can also apply varying forms of data warehouse architecture based on their data needs, scalability as well as analytical workloads.

1. Single-Tier Architecture

The single-level architecture is the least complicated type of data warehouse architecture. According to the method, everything is centralized to one database where the information is gathered on various sources. This architecture also minimizes redundancy and also simplifies the overall system design, but it is typically only applicable to small scale environments where there is limited data processing power needed.

2. Two-Tier Architecture

Two-tier architecture puts an intermediate staging zone between the source systems and the data warehouse. In this architecture, the data is initially extracted and processed in the staging area and then it is stored in the warehouse. The data warehouses are linked to analytical tools to carry out reporting and analysis. Although this architecture enhances the preparation and organization of data, it can be scaled when dealing with large volumes of data.

3. Three-Tier Architecture

Three-tier architecture is the commonest model that is commonly used in data warehouse. It divides the system into three layers; the low tier, the middle tier, and the upper tier.

The bottom level has the data warehouse database and staging processes in which raw data of various sources is cleansed, integrated and stored. ETL/ELT processes put the data into analytical format.

The middle layer includes OLAP servers which transform the data that it holds to formats that are used to make analytical queries. OLAP systems store data in multidimensional format that enables users to carry out different operations like drill-down, roll-up, slicing and dicing.

The highest level is the top-end tools and user interfaces which enables analysts and decision makers to enter the warehouse. These are reporting systems, dashboards, business intelligence platforms and other analytical applications that are used to provide insights with the data stored.

4. Cloud Data Warehouse Architecture.

As cloud computing has expanded, data warehouse architecture has become popular in many organizations due to the use of cloud architecture. The storage systems and infrastructure is hosted on the cloud platform as opposed to on-premises hardware. Cloud data warehouses offer pay-as-you-use, flexible computing, and unlimited storage.

Cloud environments allow organizations to process large volumes of structured, semi-structured, and unstructured data while scaling storage and computing resources as required. Cloud data warehouse systems often integrate with data integration services, analytical tools, and business intelligence platforms, enabling organizations to manage and analyze large datasets efficiently.

1.1.3 Limitations of Traditional Data Platforms

Organizations have been using the traditional data platforms, which include relational databases and data war0065houses to store, manage, and analyze enterprise data. These systems were initially created to support transactional and reporting loads as well as structured data. Nevertheless, as a result of the rapid digitization of technologies and the formation of data, nowadays many organizations work with a very large amount of data of different types, including web application, sensors, mobile devices, and social sites. Consequently, the conventional data platforms fail to address the requirements of the current data environment in most cases.

The other significant weakness of classical data platforms is lack of scalability. The traditional systems are based on centralized architecture and on-premise architecture. As the amount of data is growing, the organizations have to scale the hardware resources in terms of storage systems, processors, and memory. This is both costly and time-intensive, and it may need upgrades or downtime to the system. With the ever-increasing volume of data, it is also becoming more and more challenging to scale traditional platforms to support large datasets and complicated workloads of analysis.

The other drawback is the strict schema that is employed by the traditional databases and data warehouses. Such systems usually need data that conforms to a set schema before they can be stored. Although this design is effective with structured data, it would be difficult to operate within a semi-structured or unstructured environment as required by organizations where data takes the form of a text document, images, videos, or sensor data. Data processing can be slowed down and reduce the flexibility since there is the need to convert or restructure data before it can be stored.

The conventional data platforms are similarly problematic with respect to the performance of the data systems in terms of large and multifaceted datasets. With the increase in the volume of data, query processing and analytics could slow down. Most of the conventional systems are designed to process batch data as opposed to real-time data analysis, and this may slow the provision of the insights. These limitations in performance have the potential to lower the effectiveness of traditional data platforms in the contemporary business world where timely decision-making is crucial.

The other important problem is data integration. Data warehousing will frequently be based on elaborate Extract, Transform and Load (ETL) operations to gather and prepare data stored across various operational fabrications, and subsequently placing it in a centralized storage location. The procedures that are entailed in their management can be extremely complex and resource-intensive, particularly when the organizations are integrating the information of numerous sources. Such processes also need to have data consistency, accuracy, and quality among them.

Other than technical limitations, the traditional data platforms tend to be expensive to deploy and operate. Organizations have to invest in hardware facilities, database applications, storage facilities, and expertise to control and maintain the data environment. On the one hand, such systems are becoming more and more expensive and complicated to maintain as more data and analytical requirements are required.

Due to such constraints, such as scaling, inflexible data models, bottlenecks in performance, intricate integration cycles, and high operational expenses, traditional data platforms do not usually support modern data-intensive applications. These issues have pushed companies to use more recent technologies like distributed data processing systems, cloud-based database, and big data systems that are more flexible, scalable, and efficient in terms of large-scale data analytics.

1.2 Role of Data Platforms in Modern Enterprises

Data has emerged to be one of the most organizational assets in the contemporary enterprises. Companies in any sector have access to massive amounts of data due to digital transactions, online transactions, networked devices, and systems of operation. This data is critical to be managed in order to ensure that an organization is competitive in a highly dynamic digital landscape. Data platforms offer the technological support through which organizations can gather, store, process, as well as analyze data in large amounts in an organized and efficient way.

Modern data platforms are very important to aid in data-driven decision-making. Organizations are increasingly using analytical knowledge gained through enterprise data as opposed to only intuition or limited reports. Combining data with various sources and offering sophisticated analytics, data platforms can assist companies in noticing patterns, trends, and opportunities which may be used to develop strategies and operations. These applications allow companies to create meaningful insights that develop out of raw data and lead to enhanced business results.

The other significant purpose of data platforms is that they facilitate cross-departmental collaboration in an enterprise. In a massive organization, there are usually several teams of people working on the data, including finance, marketing, operations, and customer support. Data platforms are centralized or integrated environments where data can be accessed and shared amid the stakeholders safely. It will enhance transparency, the coordination among teams and also guarantees the decision-makers the availability of uniform and trustworthy information.

Big data and analytics can also help enhance innovative technology like artificial intelligence, machine learning, and predictive analytics. These technologies have become more and more popular in modern enterprises to automate operations, customize customer experience, identify risks and enhance operational efficiency. Data platforms enable organizations to scale training models, analyze complex data and deploy intelligent applications at scale by offering scalable infrastructure and end-to-end data management functionality.

Due to the ongoing digital transformation of industries, data platforms have become more comprehensive than the mere data storage systems. They are currently used as strategic infrastructures which aid innovation, business intelligence and real- time analytics. The companies managing to use the modern data systems are better placed to adapt to the market changes, automate the business processes, and create new data-driven products and services.

1.2.1 Supporting Data-Driven Decision Making

One of the approaches is data-driven decision-making (DDDM), which focuses on making business decisions based on data and analysis rather than intuition. It entails using data sources whereby customer feedback, market trends, and financial data are used to inform the decision-making process. Through the collection, analysis and interpretation of data, the organizations are able to make superior decisions that are more aligned to the business goals and objectives.

There is a daily production of more than 402.74 million terabytes of data produced by humans. When gathered and analyzed, this mass of data can help businesses make effective decisions that help reach organizational objectives and enhance customer experiences. The use of data-driven decision-making enables companies to produce real-time knowledge and forecasts as well as maximize their performance and experiment with new lines of action. These informed decisions will result in sustainable growth and profitability and basing decisions on intuition only would augment uncertainty in decision-making. Information, consequently, gives a very good basis of decision making and enhances confidence in the business strategies.

Improved customer engagement, operational efficiency, and strategic planning are some of the common areas that are improved by organizations that embrace a data-driven approach. Through customer data analysis, organizations will be able to create specific marketing campaigns and personal services which will increase customer satisfaction. Businesses can also use data analytics to decipher user behavior, preferences as well as consumption trends and organizations can enhance products and services.

Predictive analytics also enhances decision making based on data because it enables organizations to be aware of trends, risks, and opportunities. Machine learning algorithms are applied to financial institutions to identify and deter fraud through analysis of high volumes of transaction data. Equally, businesses in other industries like energy, manufacturing and supply chain management use big amounts of data about operations to forecast demand trends and the efficient utilization of resources.

Strategic planning and business development is also supported with data insights. Through demographic data, market trends, and operational data, organizations are able to determine the potential markets, business opportunities and enhance decision making in regards to investment and expansion strategies. Data analysis is also important in assisting organizations in streamlining their operations like handling stock, demand and supply chain.

Although this has many benefits, data-driven decision making has a number of challenges to implement. Bad data quality may result in a wrong analysis and wrong decisions. Within most organizations, data is captured in various systems and forms among departments and therefore it is not easy to consolidate and analyze it. The lack of data literacy may also be associated with the fact that employees do not have the required skills to analyze and utilize the data properly.

1.2.2 Integration and Management of Enterprise Data

Enterprise Data Integration refers to the act of integrating data of different sources within an organization like databases, applications, cloud systems as well as legacy systems into a single homogeneous view. It is not merely a question of transferring data in one system to another but it can be said that information across departments, systems, and technologies can be made to coordinate easily. Enterprise data integration assists organizations to establish a stable platform of reporting, analytics and enterprise activities by aligning and harmonizing data across systems.

In its essence, enterprise data integration is used to disaggregate data silos which are common in large organizations. When the information is spread out in various systems and departments it becomes hard to get the full picture of the activities in the organization. By integrating those systems, the organizations will be able to build a united data space where all the information related to various sources could be accessed and analyzed. This single perspective would allow making more accurate reports, simplify operations, and strengthen the use of analytics, artificial intelligence, and real-time decision-making.

Integration of data may be carried out using a number of methods depending on the requirements of the organizations and the environments of the systems. Application integration is the process of associating enterprise applications in a way that they can be used to share information automatically enabling updates made in one system to be transferred to others. Data consolidation refers to the process of combining data of several sources in centralized repositories like data warehouses or data lakes using operations like Extract, Transform and Load (ETL). Data propagation facilitates the constant synchronization of information in between systems such that various platforms have equal and current data.

Data virtualization is another method, where a single real-time view of the data of various distributed sources is provided without physical movement of data. In this implementation, a query layer will be asked the source systems and display the findings as a unit dataset. Another method of integration employed by modern enterprises is to use hybrid integration that is a combination of on-premises and cloud-based integration services, which helps link legacy infrastructure to the new digital platform.

In addition to data integration, the companies need to pay attention to the efficient enterprise data management. Enterprise Data Management (EDM) is the art of managing, controlling, and maximizing organizational information during the lifecycle that is, the creation and collection of data, integration of data, use of data, and ultimate archiving or disposition of data. The goal of EDM is to have the enterprise data accurate, available, safe, and in connection with the business objectives.

With the ever-growing world of data in various industries, organizations are finding it harder to keep the quality of the data, the ability to comply with regulations and guarantee timely access to information and meaningful insights out of the data volumes. Enterprise data management offers the framework and tools that would be required to handle this complexity and convert data into a useful organizational resource.

It is also important to have proper data management to serve modern technologies: artificial intelligence, machine learning, and advanced analytics. Organizations can be unable to implement intelligent systems or can create credible insights without effectively managed and incorporated data. Enterprise data integration and management can enable organizations to establish a robust data base upon which innovation, operational efficiency and data driven decision making can be achieved in contemporary enterprise settings.

1.2.3 Enabling Advanced Analytics and Artificial Intelligence

Contemporary data platforms have been key contributors to the advanced analytics and artificial intelligence in contemporary businesses. These providers offer flexible architectures, can support a wide range of data types and offer integrated tools that enable organizations to easily build, train, and deploy machine learning models. Modern data platforms have several architectural and operational characteristics, which make them viable in supporting large-scale analytics and AI-driven applications.

The first one is flexibility in architecture. Traditional warehouses are schema on write based. You make the choices in advance of how the information is to appear, and then you get it loaded. That model remains useful in the case of stable, but reporting-intensive, applications, but is limiting when you need to ingest new sources fast or allow experimentation.

The current data lake and Lakehouse move a portion of such choice to schema on read. Raw data may be stored in various forms and structure added when it is used. This simplifies it significantly to onboard sources of varying maturity, or to serve many different use cases off the same underlying data without having to redesign it all over again.

The second is the ability to support dissimilar varieties of data. Perfect relational tables are rarely used as AI workloads. They require structured data, semi-structured data like JSON, XML, and unstructured data like documents, text, and images. A contemporary platform is designed to take all that in, not as exceptions, but as the regular input.

The third aspect is ownership. In older models, one central team will be in charge of virtually all what occurs in the warehouse. Business rules are also hard coded in ETL jobs and all change requests must pass through the same tight door. This is not scalable with an increase in the use cases.

The concept of data mesh is pervading modern platforms. Data is managed as a product and control has been brought nearer to the domain. The ownership of the HR data products, supply chain data products, etc. belong to the HR and supply chain respectively. These teams establish the definition of good to the area that they take care of, they uphold the business logic, and quality is their responsibility. The platform crew supplies norms, equipment's, and railings.

The fourth is the governance, observability, and security. You desire one location where one can observe the data that is available, its definition, its origin and who is allowed to access it. You also desire finer access control and monitoring, which gives you an indicator of how new and sound each data product is in time.

The last piece is self-service. A platform is only useful if people can actually work with it. Modern data platforms are built so that analysts, data scientists, and power users can find and request the data they need, prepare it, and combine it without opening a ticket for every step. Active metadata, search, and intuitive interfaces are just as important as raw processing power.

AI does not have that context. If the input data is incomplete, inconsistent, or not available at the right time, the model will simply reflect that. There is no human intuition to correct for it. That is why the state of the data platform has such a direct impact on AI initiatives.

Data quality and availability are not abstract concerns. The absence of a modern, well-governed data platform can slow down AI development and put many initiatives at risk. A modern data platform removes structural obstacles so that teams can focus on models, use cases, and business change instead of dealing with fragmented data systems.

Data platforms are not just repositories for storing data. They are integrated ecosystems that support advanced analytics and machine learning. Many data platforms come with built-in machine learning libraries and frameworks. This enables seamless integration between data storage, processing, and model training.

This integration simplifies the workflow for data scientists. It allows them to train, validate, and deploy AI models within the same environment. Additionally, data platforms often provide support for tools such as feature stores, experiment tracking systems, and model registries. This supports collaborative development environments and helps organizations follow MLOps practices for managing machine learning systems.

1.2.4 Improving Operational Efficiency and Business Innovation

Data platforms are becoming an increasingly important part of modern enterprises to enhance efficiency and business innovation. Organizations can have a global perspective of their activities by combining information of various systems and departments. The integrated environment enables decision-makers to study trends more efficiently and make sound decisions based on the organizational objectives. When all the information of various business functions is linked and available, organizations can act much faster in response to operations issues and market opportunities.

Data platforms also assist in optimizing the business operations such as cutting down data silos and lessening redundancy of data entry to various systems. Once the information of various applications is integrated and made available real-time, then employees will be in position to obtain the information they require without having to alternate among various systems. It enhances the efficiency of workflow and allows teams to plan the activities more efficiently. Indicatively, by combining operational data provided by inventory systems, client orders and logistics operations, the organization is able to monitor activities in real time, enhance the coordination of activities across the departments.

The second major advantage is that it improves the quality and consistency of data. Organizational errors can be minimized and different records are kept when the data in various systems is combined and checked. Consistent and reliable data helps organizations to carry out correct analysis and create credible insights that can help the organization make improvements in its operations. Good quality data also enhances the business operations and will guarantee that workers and decision-makers are operating using reliable data.

The rapid reporting and analysis are also facilitated by data platforms. By having integrated and consolidated data, organizations are able to produce reports, measure performance indicators and trends more rapidly. The possibility to access information in real-time enables businesses to recognize the working inefficiencies, address the changes in the market and modify the strategies depending on the situation. By being able to interpret the information fast, such a capability increases the agility of the organization and makes evidence-based decisions more responsive.

Besides enhancing the efficiency in the operations, data platforms facilitate innovation as they allow organizations to explore novel concepts and create data-driven innovations. By combining the data of various business units like sales, marketing and customer service, organizations will be able to have a total picture of the customer behavior and business performance. Such an understanding enables the companies to create new products and services, enhance customer experiences, and exploit new market opportunities.

The cooperation between departments is also enhanced by integrated data environments. By granting access to a shared data environment to teams all over the organization, the organization can organize its activities and exchange insights and efforts towards achieving similar goals. This teamwork atmosphere facilitates the ongoing enhancement and promotes innovations through the contributions of various teams in giving their views and experience.

Lastly, the current data platforms promote scalability and long-term expansion of the organization. The integrated data systems enable the addition of new sources of data to the system without interfering with the business activities as the business grows and the data generated increases. The scalability means that the organizations would be able to keep optimizing processes, meet the new business demands, and remain competitive in the ever-data-driven economy.

1.3 Emergence of Cloud-Based Data Platforms

The high pace of the development of digital technologies and the growing amount of information generated by contemporary businesses have revolutionized how organizations handle and process information. The legacies of on-premises data platforms, which proved to be efficient over many years, are not always able to address the requirements of the new data environment that requires extensive storage, an ability to quickly and flexibly process data, and quicker access to insights. With the arrival of cloud computing technologies in organizations, cloud-based data platforms were introduced as another way of managing and analyzing enterprise data.

Cloud-based data platforms are cloud infrastructure-based services that are scalable and offer storage, computing and data management services via the internet. Organizations are able to store and process data in distributed clouds through the use of cloud service providers instead of having physical servers and hardware within their premises. The change enables companies to have access to the powerful data processing capabilities without necessarily having to make expensive investments in hardware and infrastructure.

Scalability and flexibility of cloud-based data platforms is one of the key benefits of these solutions. Cloud environments enable organizations to increase storage and computing capacity as required in line with the needs of the organization thereby making them to be able to manage the increasing amounts of data effectively. Cloud platforms are extremely dynamic in addressing the needs of the business since businesses can add or remove resources depending on the workload.

A large variety of contemporary data technologies such as big data analytics, artificial intelligence, machine learning, and real-time data processing are also supported by cloud-based data platforms. Through the capabilities incorporated into cloud infrastructures, organizations can create sophisticated data pipelines, create models to analyze their data, and create insights on large data volumes faster than with the traditional systems.

Other benefits of cloud-based platforms include less infrastructure management, enhanced collaboration as well as accelerated release of data solutions in addition to scalability and the ability to perform advanced analytics. The cloud service providers provide data storage, processing and analytics managed services enabling an organization to invest more in the data led innovation than in the upkeep of a complicated IT infrastructure.

Cloud-based data platforms have become an essential part of the contemporary enterprise architecture as digital transformation is happening across the industries. Companies are growing more dependent on big data environments, which are managed on these platforms, to support sophisticated analytics applications and allow decision-making based on data in a fast-changing technological environment.

1.3.1 Drivers Behind the Adoption of Cloud-Based Data Platforms

The implementation of cloud-based data platforms has risen tremendously as companies are being subjected to increased pressures of scalable data storage, rapid analytics, and scalable infrastructure. The old on-premises systems can hardly cope with immense data that is generated by contemporary digital applications, interconnected devices, and web services. With businesses becoming more and more dependent on data in making decisions and driving innovation, cloud-based systems have become a viable option in data storage, processing and analytics of enterprise data.

Scalability and flexibility is one of the leading factors that have resulted in the use of cloud-based data platforms. Cloud services enable an organization to add or subtract computing and storage capabilities based on current workload demands. This elasticity allows the businesses to manage the growing datasets and changing processing needs without requiring the investment in new physical hardware. Through dynamic resource allocation, organizations have the capability of sustaining performance in the management of big and complex data environments.

Another reason why organizations should consider using cloud data platforms is cost efficiency. The traditional data infrastructure needs a considerable amount of investments in servers, storage systems, networking equipment, and the maintenance of the data center. Cloud computing lowers these initial infrastructure expenses by availing the resources either in subscription or pay-as-you-use. In this approach the organizations can convert the high capital expenditures into operational costs and they can manage their budgets on technology.

The shift to data platforms relying on clouds also plays a major role in business agility and faster innovation. Cloud computing also enables organizations to install data services and data analytical tools in a very fast manner and it takes a lesser duration to install new technologies and data solutions. This type of flexibility prepares an enterprise to react more quickly to the new trends in the business, experiment with new data applications, and create new data-driven products and services.

The other critical force is the ability to centralize and improve interaction between teams of an organization. The data stored on cloud platforms can be maintained and operated in centralized areas, which could be accessed in other locations. This kind of accessibility enables inter-departmental teams to work on the same data sets that improves collaboration and accessibility of consistent and current information by decision-makers.

The accelerated growth of the application of complex analytics, big data technologies, and artificial intelligence also led to the creation of cloud-based data platforms. The analytical needs of the present day include not only the possession of strong computing power but also the ability to work with the data of enormous volume and different types. Clouds provide scalable computing environment and inbuilt analytics that has the potential of supporting such complex analytical requirements.

1.3.2 Key Features and Advantages of Cloud Data Platforms

A number of fundamental features of cloud data platforms make them highly advantageous over conventional ways of data management.

- **Scalability and elasticity:** Scalability and elasticity is one of the greatest benefits of cloud data platforms which is inherent. These systems have automated scaling features and this enables organizations to scale their storage and compute capabilities up or down on demand.
- **Strong security**: Security is the most important aspect of any data management system and cloud data platforms have all-encompassing security features, which ensure protection of sensitive information. These networks have many layers of security, which can also involve the encryption of data, identity and access management (IAM) and compliance certification (to regulations such as HIPAA, GDPR, etc.).
- **Real-time data processing and analytics**: The ability to process and analyze data on the fly as it is being generated is becoming more and more a requirement of modern businesses in order to be able to get a timely insight and respond to the changing conditions as fast as possible. Cloud data platforms have the capability to receive real-time data streams of different kinds, including internet of things devices, applications and online transactions.

    - **Integration and interoperability:** Cloud data platforms are designed to be easily integrated with many other cloud platform services as well as on-premises systems. Those are data integration tools, business intelligence platforms, and AI/ML services among other applications. This interoperability assists in ensuring that information flows freely within the organization to enable one to have a unified picture of the information in the organization.
    - **Cost-effectiveness:** The pay-as-you-go pricing models of the cloud data solutions have high-cost advantages as compared to the capital-intensive nature of the on-premise solutions. The resources paid are not required to be big initial investment and reduces the possibility of over-provisioning because the resources that are paid are only used by organizations.

All of these aspects make cloud data platforms a decent and diverse answer to the modern data management. They are used to allow organizations to scale their data operations, secure their data, obtain real-time insights, as well as innovate cost-effectively.

Cloud data platforms reduce the pressure of data management and allow organizations to store, secure and manipulate data in a more intuitive way as compared to the traditional ways. These benefits include:

- **Enhanced agility**

  Cloud data platforms enable organizations to quickly release and scale data services as required. The process of acquiring and installing new infrastructure can take a long time, which is removed with the on-demand nature of cloud resources. This enables businesses to be flexible to new market conditions, trial new data initiatives and deliver data-driven products and services to the market in a shorter time.

- **Improved scalability and performance**

  As mentioned previously, the scalability nature of cloud platforms can guarantee that organizations can support a growing amount of data and an increased analytical load without the risk of performance being the capacity problem. The dynamic capacity to provision compute and storage power enables large datasets and complicated queries to be effectively handled.

- **Cost optimization**

  The pay-as-you-go pricing system of cloud data provider translates into high-cost savings. Companies do not spend significant capital initial outlays on hardware and software: they just pay on the resources used.

- **Greater availability and cooperation**

  Cloud data platforms put data and analytics tools at reach anywhere on the internet connection. This promotes teamwork in distributed teams, and enables users throughout the organization to use data as per their requirements. Self-service analytics also make data more democratic and eliminate the need to deploy expert IT teams just to get a first-level report and analysis.

- **Automated Backup**

  Automated backup schedules are enjoyed by organizations that have a cloud data platform. This will ensure that their precious data is frequently backed up and therefore the chances of data loss caused by human factor, hardware failure or other unforeseen occurrences are far lowered.

1.3.3 Impact of Cloud Data Platforms on Modern Data Architectures

Data platforms that run on the cloud have played a major role in the development of contemporary data architectures. With the growing use of cloud infrastructure by organizations to store and process large amounts of data, the traditional data management methods started to change in order to become more scalable, flexible and able to meet a wide range of analytical needs. This revolution saw the development of modern data architectures that include the benefits of the previous data management systems but exploit the benefits of cloud-based technologies.

The architectures, which characterize the last decade, are not substitutes of the past, they are developments. Organizations continue to use data warehouses, data lakes, and other known modeling tools, but such technologies have evolved and become more interconnected with an ecosystem. With time it was already evident that it is not possible to find one solution to all data management demands and each technology has its purpose and its merits and downsides.

With the development of cloud platforms, the previously distinct concepts started combining. The edge between structured and unstructured data, storage and compute began to become unclear. This change led to the Modern Data Warehouse, where the governance and performance of the traditional warehouse is merged with the flexibility and scalability of the data lake.

The modern data warehouse came as a result of the experience with the huge data lakes. Although data lakes were more flexible, cost-efficient, organizations found that they were not always structured, governed, and reliable to support business-critical analytics. Meanwhile, classical data warehouses were not able to process the heterogeneity and vast amounts of contemporary business data. The Data warehouse The Modern Data Warehouse fills this gap by integrating data lake flexibility with the structure and control of the data warehouse.

The data lake will serve as a staging and exploration environment in this architecture, as the point of entry of various and fast-changing data sources. The data warehouse serves as the serving and governance layer, which assumes the responsibility of security and compliance, as well as uniform reporting. This architecture combines the schema-on-write discipline of the warehouse and the schema-on-read flexibility of the lake, enabling a broad spectrum of analytics to both the exploratory data science and the controlled business reporting.

The mature query optimization methods that have been used in data warehouses to speed up data retrieval and guarantee response predictability with large datasets have included the use of indexing, partitioning, and materialized views. These optimization features together with the popular SQL interface have enabled data warehouses to become formidable as well as user friendly by analysts and business users. With this integration, organizations will be able to operate at a higher pace and analyze data in an efficient manner. The data stored in the lake can be used by data scientists to build and deploy models and analysts and business users to work with curated datasets in the warehouse.

Although these are the benefits, new varieties of complexity also came with the Modern Data Warehouse. The maintenance of various storage and processing systems will add more overhead to the operations and make it harder to govern. Lakes and warehouses tend to duplicate data and this may result in data silos. Such silos arise when the departments construct their unique pipelines, or when the same information is processed differently across its locations of storage.

Such fragmentation may compromise the process of establishing a unified and trusted data base in the long run. Measurements can be inaccurate, inter-team work can be slow down, and wisdom may be trapped in a particular tool or department. The other potential problem is that it has a high level of integration with cloud-native services which may lead to higher reliance on one vendor and complicate system migration.

Combined with the increasing requirement of real-time analytics, simplified architecture and single governance, these issues gave rise to the next leap in the history of data platforms. The Data Lakehouse architecture was created to solve these problems by incorporating the flexibility of data lakes and the reliability and governance of data warehouses on the same platform.

1.4 Transition from On-Premise to Cloud Infrastructures

Moving the on-premise infrastructure to the cloud-based environment is one of the biggest changes of the current data management. Conventionally, companies used to use on-premise data centers in order to store and handle enterprise data. These systems have forced businesses to buy, install and maintain their own hardware and software infrastructure such as server, storage systems, network equipment and database management systems. Although this offered organizations direct control over their data environments, it was also an expensive strategy that demanded a lot of capital investment and maintenance.

As the volume of data grew and business need started to get complicated, much of the organizations started to feel constrained by on-premise infrastructure. Expansion of traditional systems was traditionally associated with the need to buy new hardware and upgrade current data center facilities, which might be both expensive and time-consuming. Moreover, running systems on-premise needed specific IT departments to maintain infrastructure, update systems, and protect and maintain them.

Cloud computing brought a different way of looking at data infrastructure because it enables organizations to utilize computing resource by outsourcing them to cloud service provider instead of having physical systems that are owned and operated in their premises. In the cloud, storage of data, processing power, and networking facilities are provided by remote data centers that are under the management of cloud providers. With this model, organizations are able to access the infrastructural resources, whenever they are needed, via the internet.

Scalability can be regarded as one of the main benefits of cloud infrastructure. Cloud solutions enable companies to increase or decrease computing and storage resources according to the needs of their operation. Organizations are able to dynamically allocate resources as the need arises instead of buying hardware to support expansion in the future, thereby enhancing efficiency and decreasing infrastructure expenses.

One more significant advantage of cloud infrastructure is that it allows for minimizing the infrastructure management tasks. Some of the tasks that cloud providers carry out include system maintenance, hardware maintenance and monitoring infrastructure. This enables organizations to concentrate more on creating applications, data analysis and creating business value instead of operating complicated IT infrastructure.

The transition into cloud infrastructure also leads to increased agility of the organization. Business organizations can deploy new applications, data pipelines, data analytics solutions, and faster than on-premise systems with the aid of cloud platforms. This flexibility allows organizations to experiment with various emerging technologies such as artificial intelligence, machine learning, and real time analytics without the need to invest heavily to get the infrastructure ready.

1.4.1 Types of Cloud Migration

1. P2V (Physical to Virtual)

P2V (Physical to Virtual) migration is a method to move your on-premises stuff to the cloud. You change your servers and data into virtual machines that you can use on cloud platforms like Amazon Web Services (AWS), Microsoft Azure, or Google Cloud.

To do a successful P2V migration, you need to plan and assess your inventory. Organisations must know their servers, storage devices, network parts, and software applications. They must choose what should be moved to the virtual environment.

2. P2C (Physical to Cloud)

P2C, or Physical to Cloud migration, involves transferring your physical infrastructure to cloud-based servers. It is more common now because it's cheaper and less complicated to manage. The P2C process often includes making an inventory of applications and deciding which ones work in the cloud.

The migration might need to refactor code and move applications to a new environment. You may replace things that don't work with the new platform or move them to the cloud with no significant changes - this is called lift-and-shift.

P2C can give you speed and flexibility while saving money on capital expenses (CapEx) and operating expenses (OpEx). Once you move to the cloud using transition services like AWS Database Migration Service, you must follow compliance rules like HIPAA and GDPR.

3. 2V (Virtual to Virtual)

V2V (Virtual to Virtual) migration involves transferring virtual machines from one virtualisation environment to another. It is a popular method used for migrating on-premise infrastructure to the cloud.

The type of migration may save time, resources and minimize the risks that are experienced in the old hardware migrations. It maintains your settings, applications and data.

As an example, businesses that are on VMware are able to migrate their VMs directly on VMware Cloud on AWS with V2V migration. It is an effective process that ensures order needed to be compatible with already existing systems. During this type of cloud migration, the testing and checking are necessary. You must have a plan and do everything to avoid interruptions.

4. V2C (Virtual to Cloud)

V2C or Virtual to Cloud migration refers to the shift of virtual machines on the local infrastructure to cloud providers. The companies apply this to migrate their digital systems to a conveniently scalable and easy-to-use cloud system.

Equally, MongoDB to Snowflake migration is another case of Virtual to Cloud migration where by the companies frequently use database migration tools to migrate their database systems out of virtualized databases to cloud-based data warehouses to support better scalability and enhanced analytics.

1.4.2 Benefits of Migrating to the Cloud

- **Increased Accessibility**

  Accessibility is one of the major advantages of migrating to the cloud. In the case of on-premise infrastructure, access to data and applications is only available based on physical location or outdated hardware. However, cloud infrastructure lets you use data anywhere and anytime, needing only an internet connection.

Take a financial institution with offices in various regions needing real-time access to customer data. These branches can easily access customer info by shifting their systems to the cloud.

Also, cloud-based tools like unified communication platforms let employees work together effectively, no matter where they are.

- **Improved Performance and Agility**

  Migrating to the cloud can improve a company's performance and agility. It provides faster access to resources, allowing for quick changes and updates.

  Cloud migration offers flexible deployment options. It includes hybrid multi-cloud systems or on-premises solutions without being locked in.

- **Elasticity And Scalability**

  A significant benefit of migrating to the cloud is elasticity and scalability. With on-site infrastructure, scaling up or down needs hardware changes that can be costly and time-consuming.

  The cloud lets businesses quickly grow and shrink their resources in response to changes in demand.

- **Cost Efficiency**

  There is a saving of cost in migrating to the cloud. You can do away with hardware, maintenance, and electricity bills because you have left behind on-premises infrastructure. Cloud providers are able to provide different pricing schemes, such as the pay-as-you-go and consumption-based pricing. These alternatives are easy to manage costs yet obtain the highest quality analytic tools.

5. Increased Security and Compliance.

It is more secure and compliant than on-site infrastructure because of migrating to the cloud. Cloud service providers (CSPs) spend a great deal of money and time on actual security mechanisms to secure the information of clients. Cloud solutions have powerful analytics and lower cost of ownership, all while guarding your data.

1.4.3 Cloud Migration Challenges

1. Lack Of Cloud Migration Strategy

A cloud migration strategy is among the top challenges of on-premise to cloud migration. Many organisations need to plan better for cloud migration, leading to costly mistakes and disruptions.

To mitigate this risk, experts suggest creating an inventory detailing all applications that interact with each other. Work with corporate customers or partners before beginning the migration planning process.

2. Managing Costs

One of the biggest challenges in on-premise to cloud migration is cost management. Moving to the cloud can often involve many hidden costs. It may include data transfer fees and ongoing operational expenses.

Another issue with on-premise to cloud migration is managing costs, as there can be hidden costs. It is essential to examine the total cost of ownership (TCO) for each workload planned for migration. See whether the cost of transitioning to the clouds will be less expensive.

3. Vendor Lock-Ins

The vendor lock-in may prevent the migration of organisations to the cloud. The issue arises when a firm over depends on a particular CSP or technology, and changing it would be rather challenging and expensive.

It is important to make the right selection of cloud service provider and technology stack. The flexibility of the open-source technology makes it a good choice and it can be applied to the other cloud platform.

4. Information Security and Governance.

There may be data compliance and security issues between on-premise and cloud environments. Moving sensitive data to a new platform would be potentially unsafe and risky in terms of regulation.

During the migration to the cloud, compliance issues such as GDPR, HIPAA, and PCI-DSS should be taken into account. A properly conducted risk evaluation prior to migration contributes to the detection of the possible vulnerabilities that would be dealt with in advance.

1.4.4 Step-by-Step Cloud Migration Process

1. Set a Migration Architect Role

The establishment of the Migration Architect position is one of the most important aspects of a successful on-premises to cloud migration. The individual leads and implements the migration plan and makes sure that all the elements are consistent with the business objectives and performance targets.

2. Select your Level of Cloud Integration.

Businesses should make a decision on the extent of cloud integration when they migrate to the cloud.

Moving to the cloud can be done in two ways; shallow integration and deep integration. Shallow refers to the act of uprooting everything but leaving it to the same as it was before. It is cheaper and faster but can potentially only provide part of the advantages of the cloud.

Deep integration implies that you make changes to make your applications more effective in the cloud, and you save money in the long run.

3. Multi-Cloud Strategy or Single Cloud.

In migrating to the cloud, you have an option of a single provider or numerous providers. One is more convenient to use but may be restrictive. With many, you have a greater choice and greater security, but it also involves more work.

4. Establish Cloud KPIs And Performance Baselines.

It is important to establish KPIs and performance baselines to gauge the effectiveness of cloud migration.

Before relocating, determine what you want to improve such as your speed of loading a web site. It will assist you in monitoring your progress and ensure that your move is fruitful.

5. Migration Components Should Be a Priority.

Practice pre-empting the components that you need to adopt in transitioning to the cloud. It can be a core system such as core operations of a bank, authentication of a bank by the customer by use of passkeys or the most valuable information.

Assess which data needs to be migrated based on its importance and urgency for day-to-day operations.

6. Perform Refactoring

Refactoring involves optimizing an application's existing code for the cloud environment. It helps increase performance and reduce costs by making applications more efficient, scalable, and resilient.

One example of refactoring includes modifying an application to work effectively with various running instances. It enables applications to move from a monolithic architecture to one that utilizes distributed microservices. You get flexibility and agility in the cloud environment.

7. Create a Data Migration Plan

A good plan for moving your data is critical. Take stock of everything you have and then move it securely to the cloud. Then, update your old systems to work better in your new home.

8. Switch Over Production

Once the necessary preparation and testing are complete, switching to production is time. To reduce the risk of issues, test everything in stages before switching.

1.5 Challenges of Managing Large-Scale Data

Big data is more than just information in large quantities—more specifically, it's data too large and complex to manage or process with conventional methods. Processing even a fraction of the millions of terabytes of data generated daily takes considerable computing power and storage capacity. It also takes data quality, data management, and data analytics expertise to maintain all that data and unlock its potential.

Even a minor amount of data can be helpful to businesses that know how to use it to learn more about customer behavior, product performance, and market trends, for example—but small volumes of data also provide limited reliability. Just as a larger sample size ensures scientific experiments are more representative of the real world, big data provides a better look into actual events and trends.

The Big Data "3 Vs"

The "big" in big data covers three primary categories, known as the Three V's—volume, velocity, and variety:

- **Volume.** This is the most straightforward of the three, as big data naturally involves huge amounts of data. The sheer scale of information in these datasets renders conventional storage and management systems effectively useless.
- **Velocity.** Big data is also big in its velocity, or how fast new information is gathered and processed. Processing must be rapid to keep up with the pace of information.
- **Variety.** information in these data sets comes in multiple formats from numerous sources—industrial devices, social media channels, emails, for example—and can include text, sales data, videos, pictures, or sensor information, to name just a few. This rich variety provides a more complete picture of what the business wants to understand.

These three dimensions provide a useful way to think about big data and the challenges of working with it. It involves unthinkably huge amounts of data coming in like a firehose at blistering speeds in too many shapes and sizes to easily manage.

1.5.1 Cybersecurity and Privacy

The security and the privacy of sensitive information is one of the greatest problems in management of large-scale data environment. Organizations that gather and process mass data are likely to have stored personal, financial, and operation information that should not be accessed by third parties. Cyber threat attacks have a larger and larger attack surface as the magnitude of data grows. Organizational systems containing a large amount of data are often targeted by cybercriminals due to the fact that such a system might hold a treasure trove of personal information, financial data, or even company secrets.

Breach of data may lead to serious monetary losses, legal fines and loss of reputation of an organization. Besides the cybersecurity threats, the organizations will also be obliged to adhere to different data protection laws like the General Data Protection Regulation (GDPR) and other privacy practices. These laws pose stringent conditions on the manner in which personal information is gathered, stored, and processed and distributed.

The large-scale management of privacy and security involves the presence of quality security architectures such as encryption, access control systems, identity management systems and continuous monitoring. There is also a need that organizations should have a clear visibility of their data assets so that organizations know what kind of data they are gathering, where it is stored and how it is utilized. Lack of proper governance and security controls can make operations and legal management of large-scale data to pose huge operational and legal threats to organizations.

1.5.2 Data Quality and Data Governance

Another significant difficulty associated with dealing with large-scale datasets is the maintenance of high data quality. The quality of data is defined as its accuracy, completeness, consistency and reliability of data that is utilized in the analysis and decision-making. With the increase in the amount of data, the probability of errors, missing values, duplications and inconsistent data formats is also likely to be found.

Inadequate data quality has the potential of greatly influencing the outcome of the analysis and making wrong decisions. Indicatively, incorrect customer information could result in poor marketing strategies whereas poor operational information could result in poor performance reports. In a world where machine learning models take knowledge of data to make predictions, compromised data quality may also bring about unreliable or bias predictions.

Strong data governance frameworks must be adopted by organizations in order to deal with these problems. Data governance is constituted of policies, standards and procedures which guarantee data is handled in the same way throughout the organization. These models specify data ownership responsibilities, data standards, and implement data validation to ensure data reliability.

Data also has to be documented, standardized and monitored in its lifecycle as ensured by effective governance. Having clear governance systems, the organizations have the opportunity to build trust on their data and facilitate credible decision-making throughout business processes.

1.5.3 Data Integration and Data Silos

Big data environments frequently incorporate data gathered by many systems, such as enterprise applications, Internet of Things devices, web platforms, and external sources of data. The combination of these heterogeneous data to one unified environment is not that easy. Various systems can be based on various data formats, storage mechanisms and communication protocols, which can result in a difficult integration.

Where integration is not addressed adequately, the data is usually confined in different systems referred to as data silos. These silos do not allow organizations to have a single perspective of their operations due to the fragmentation of information in the departments and platforms. As an example, the customer information can be kept apart in marketing systems, sales systems, customer support systems, etc and it is hard to analyze customer behavior in a comprehensive way.

Information silos restrict inter-team cooperation and lower the efficiency of analytics programs. They further complicate the process of data governance since policies and standards might not be uniformly applied in various systems.

To surmount integration issues, it is necessary to use data integration tools, standardized data pipeline, and centralized data platforms like data warehouses or data lakes. The combination of data between the systems enables organizations to generate single-system data that can be used in enterprise analytics and strategic decision-making.

Scalability of Data storage and infrastructure

Big data is very massive in size and is a source of grave problems in terms of storage capacity and infrastructure scalability. Organizations are forced to store massive amounts of data and ensure they are readily available to analytics and reporting. The traditional storage systems cannot always deal with the soaring volumes of data, especially when it concerns the production of the data that is produced in rivers out of the digital platforms, sensors and enterprise systems.

As the amount of data grows, the organizations should also be in a position to scale the infrastructure to handle the growing processing needs. The old standardized storage systems may be improved by purchasing new hardware, upgrading the data centers and allocating additional computing resources. This can be costly and time consuming to upgrade particularly when handling petabytes of data.

The other dilemma exists because organizations must choose between two competing needs which require them to decide how much data they will store. Organizations need to establish data management policies which include decisions about data retention, long-term storage, archiving, and permanent data deletion. The absence of effective data lifecycle management results in operational difficulties and financial burdens for storage systems. Companies increasingly adopt scalable architectural solutions which include distributed storage systems and cloud data storage platforms to handle their big data storage needs. These solutions offer the flexibility to store and process massive datasets and keep the performance and reliability.

Data Analysis and Interpretation Complexity

Though big-scale data can be great resources of information generation opportunities, the process of analysis and interpretation may turn out to be incredibly difficult. The nature of big data is more complex because of the volume of data as well as the variety of the data sources and rate at which data is produced.

Large datasets are not well processed using traditional analytical tools and manual methods of analysis. Analysis that should be performed to extract meaningful insights will require a high level of analytical approaches such as machine learning, artificial intelligence, and distributed computing models. The technologies enable organizations to save high amounts of data and extract trends that would not have been easily identified using the traditional means.

Nonetheless, domain knowledge and application evaluation are also needed in the interpretation of analytical results. Automated analytics systems will be able to find some correlations or trends that might be significant but not necessarily reflective of the real-world distributions. Organizations that fail to interpret and validate their decisions, engage in misleading or incomplete information when deciding on matters related to them.

The effective management of large data volumes hence demands not only sophisticated analytical systems but also highly qualified data specialists, who are able to interpret the outcomes, confirm the findings and convert the information about the data into an effective business strategy.

Multiple Choice Questions (MCQs)

1. **What was the primary purpose of traditional databases in early enterprise systems?**
   A. To support machine learning model training
   B. To store and manage structured transactional data
   C. To replace all business intelligence tools
   D. To host cloud-native applications

2. **Which of the following best describes a data warehouse?**
   A. A system used only for website hosting
   B. A repository optimized for analytical querying and reporting
   C. A tool used exclusively for mobile application development
   D. A platform for social media management

3. **What is one major difference between traditional databases and data warehouses?**
   A. Traditional databases are used for analytics, while data warehouses are used only for backups
   B. Data warehouses are designed for query-intensive analysis, while traditional databases support operational transactions
   C. Traditional databases require no storage, while data warehouses do
   D. There is no difference between them

4. **Why are data platforms considered essential in modern enterprises?**
   A. They eliminate the need for business strategies
   B. They enable organizations to store, process, and derive insights from data
   C. They are used only for employee attendance systems
   D. They reduce the need for cybersecurity

5. **Which of the following is a key advantage of modern data platforms for enterprises?**
   A. Limited access to organizational data

B. Reduced collaboration between teams
C. Faster decision-making through data-driven insights
D. Elimination of all operational costs

6. **What factor significantly contributed to the emergence of cloud-based data platforms?**
   A. Declining internet connectivity worldwide
   B. Need for scalable, flexible, and cost-efficient data management
   C. Elimination of data generation in businesses
   D. Reduced use of digital applications

7. **Which of the following is a common feature of cloud-based data platforms?**
   A. Fixed hardware capacity with no scalability
   B. Manual-only infrastructure management
   C. On-demand resource provisioning and elasticity
   D. Exclusive support for paper-based records

8. **What is a major reason organization transition from on-premise infrastructure to cloud infrastructure?**
   A. To increase dependency on physical servers
   B. To avoid remote accessibility
   C. To improve scalability, availability, and operational efficiency
   D. To reduce data accessibility for teams

9. **Which of the following is a common challenge in managing large-scale data?**
   A. Lack of any data growth in organizations
   B. Difficulty in handling data volume, variety, and velocity
   C. Complete elimination of data security concerns
   D. No need for integration across systems

10. **Why is governance important in large-scale data platform management?**

A. It prevents organizations from using data

B. It ensures data quality, security, compliance, and proper access control

C. It removes the need for data storage systems

D. It only applies to small businesses

Answers

1	2	3	4	5	6	7	8	9	10
B	B	B	B	C	B	C	C	B	B

CHAPTER 2

CLOUD DATABASES AND ARCHITECTURE

2.1 OVERVIEW OF CLOUD DATABASE MODELS

A cloud database is one that is given, deployed, and accessed on the cloud. Similar to conventional on-premises databases, cloud databases arrange and store ordered, unstructured, and semi-structured data (Hwang & Chen, 2017). They do, however, also offer many of the advantages of cloud computing, such as lower prices, speed, scalability, and agility.

Cloud databases can be categorized as relational or non-relational databases, just like conventional on-premises databases.

- **Relational Cloud database** Relational cloud databases consist of one or more tables with rows and columns that let you arrange data in predetermined relationships to understand how the data makes sense. Structured query language (SQL) can be used to query and modify data in these databases, which usually have predefined data formats. They work best with a lot of structured data and are incredibly dependable and constant.

Spanner, PostgreSQL, MySQL, Oracle, SQL Server, and Cloud SQL are examples of relational databases.

- **Non-relational cloud databases** store and handle unstructured data, including text messages from mobile devices and emails, rich media files, documents, surveys, and sensor data. Unlike relational databases, which have a strict structure, they let you store and arrange data in any format.

MongoDB, Redis, Cassandra, HBase, and Bigtable are a few non-relational database examples.

These days, the quantity of data produced and gathered is increasing at an exponential rate. It's very different, but it's also more diversified. It is currently challenging to combine using conventional methods because data may span across both remote cloud apps and services and on-premises databases. Furthermore, real-time data processing is becoming more and more crucial to business success; gaps or delays in data transmission to mission-critical applications could be catastrophic.

Legacy databases confront major issues as cloud use grows and data demand continues to change.

Flexibility, dependability, security, affordability, and more are offered by cloud databases. supplying a strong basis for the creation of contemporary commercial applications. Specifically, they are able to quickly adjust to shifting demands and workloads without adding extra work to teams that are already overburdened.

2.1.1 Advantages of Cloud Databases

- **Reduced operational overhead:** Physical infrastructure management and upkeep are eliminated by cloud databases. All of the hardware, operating systems, and database software must be provisioned, updated, and maintained by your cloud provider.
- **Improved agility and scalability:** In only a few minutes, you can start either shut down an existing cloud database or create a new one. This enables you to test, validate, and operationalise new ideas more quickly. Additionally, cloud databases can offer consistent performance under high load and dynamically scale as your apps expand.
- **Lower total cost of ownership (TCO):** Teams can concentrate on developing applications as the infrastructure is owned and operated by the cloud service provider. Pay-as-you-go alternatives also allow you to scale up or down based on your consumption and provision what you need, when you need it.
- **Flexible database options:** You can choose cloud databases created especially to satisfy your application's performance and functionality requirements and use case.
- **Safe, secure data:** In order to provide several security layers and centralised security policies that can help protect client data

without impeding innovation, cloud providers invest in the newest technology and specialists.

- **Better reliability:** High availability, automated backups, and strong disaster recovery are just a few of the built-in features that cloud platforms, particularly cloud databases, offer to ensure constant connectivity and satisfy SLAs.

2.1.2 Benefits of a Cloud Database

Numerous advantages of cloud databases are shared by other cloud services, such as:

- **Improved agility and innovation.** The quick deployment and decommissioning of cloud databases makes it easy new business models may be tested, validated, and operationalized quickly. The company can easily abandon a project (as well as its database) and move on to the next invention if it chooses not to operationalize it.
- **Faster time to market.** Using a cloud database eliminates the need to order hardware and wait for shipping, installation, or network configuration while There is a new product in the development queue. It only takes a few minutes to gain access to databases.
- **Reduced risks.** Particularly for DBaaS models, cloud databases have many chances to lower risk throughout the entire company. Cloud service providers can reduce the likelihood of human error, which is the main cause of software outages, by using automation to enforce security best practices and features. Service level agreements (SLAs) and automated high-availability features help minimize or completely eradicate revenue loss due to downtime.
- **Lower costs.** End users can plan for steady state, scale up for high demand during peak hours, then scale back down when demand returns to steady state with pay-per-use subscription models that offer dynamic scaling. Compared to keeping comparable capabilities internally, which would require businesses to buy genuine servers capable of handling peak demand even if they might only need peak capabilities on a few days each quarter, this is substantially less expensive. Simply shutting off services when not in use might help businesses save money.

Additionally, a cloud database eliminates the complexity, latency, expense, and dangers associated with extract, transform, and load (ETL) duplication by combining machine learning, real-time analytics across data lakes and warehouses, and transaction processing into a single database service.

2.1.3 Cloud Database Management Choices

Businesses can choose how to handle their cloud databases. Four broad categories can be used to classify database administration styles:

- **Self-Managed Cloud Databases:** In this strategy, a company uses a cloud infrastructure to run its database, but it administers the database itself using internal resources without the cloud vendor integrating any automation. While the firm retains accountability and control over database administration, some of the typical advantages of shifting a database to the cloud, such as increased flexibility and agility, are provided by this paradigm.
- **Automated Cloud Databases:** Under this paradigm, businesses employ application programming interfaces (APIs) for database cloud services to help with lifecycle activities, although they still have access to and control over the database servers. over operating systems and database setup. Automated database services usually don't include scheduled tasks like patching and maintenance, and therefore have restricted SLAs.
- **Managed Cloud Databases:** Even though the cloud provider does not let consumers access to the servers housing the database, this architecture is comparable to automated cloud databases. Because end users are not permitted to install their own, configuration is restricted to cloud vendor-supported options applications.
- **Autonomous Cloud Databases:** The human labour involved in database management and performance tuning is eliminated by automation and machine learning in this new, hands-free operating model. SLAs for business-Services include key applications like zero-downtime operations for planned and unforeseen database and service lifecycle activities.

2.2 Distributed Database Architecture

To increase overall system performance, scalability, and reliability, a distributed database stores data across several physical locations. These server clusters, sometimes referred to as instances or nodes, that make up a distributed database may be located in one or more data centers. They may even be hosted by many cloud providers or dispersed throughout various geographical areas.

A distributed database can grow horizontally to utilize the processing and storage power of several machines. This architecture greatly improves data availability since, in the event of a node loss, the database may easily obtain the required data from another node. High availability, data longevity, and horizontal scalability are all offered by distributed databases. They are therefore increasingly prevalent in modern application designs and architectures that support cloud-based infrastructures, globally distributed apps, and compute-intensive generative AI services.

Distributed databases are a cornerstone technology of high-throughput and high availability database systems. The primary architectural feature of these databases is a collection of networked servers, also referred to as instances or nodes, that store, update, and balance data among themselves.

Depending on the use case, a node may store a complete copy of the data or only a portion of it. Distributed systems that store a complete copy on each node are typically used for disaster recovery. The more common technique is to partition, or shard, portions of the overall data set on different nodes and then share and balance the workloads through the network. This partitioning can be done horizontally (by rows) or vertically (by columns), depending on whether the system is designed primarily for transactions or for batch analytics.

Any coordination and communication among nodes are orchestrated through a distributed database management system (DDBMS) that facilitates data consistency, handles transactions, and provides a unified view of data to users.

2.2.1 Uses of Distributed Databases

Distributed database technology is the support of modern, global claims and cloud services. Some use cases rely on NoSQL document-type databases, which are well suited to highly scalable web applications. These databases offer BASE-type (basic availability, soft state, and eventual consistency) data consistency and allow for fast, scalable transactions with eventual consistency. Other Relational databases that offer ACID (atomicity, consistency, isolation, and durability) compliance are essential for applications like those managed by international financial institutions or online merchants. This helps them provide the most immediately accurate transactions and data processing to clients and inventory control systems.

Both database architectures allow for a database to be distributed across multiple servers. The BASE databases implement a design which sacrifices immediate data consistency to achieve better system availability and scalability. The ACID system protects data integrity while ensuring system reliability which makes it suitable for financial transaction applications that require absolute data consistency.

The following list contains five of the most common examples:

1. **Scalable web applications:** Distributed databases serve as the essential backbone for web applications which must manage both extensive user traffic and substantial data processing. Document-style database architectures serve as the foundation for social media platforms and ecommerce websites and content management systems. The system enables multiple nodes to share database processing tasks which helps it maintain performance during times of increased traffic and business expansion.
2. **Big data analytics:** Big data analytics systems require real-time processing to handle their extensive data sets. The system needs a distributed database to manage storage and processing operations across multiple nodes which handle dynamic workload distribution between three main components, namely data warehouses, business intelligence applications, and machine learning systems.
3. **Geographically distributed operations:** Distributed databases enable organizations with worldwide operations to maintain consistent data access across different locations. The distributed database system enables administrators to decrease network delay times while enhancing system performance by storing data near the users or applications that require access to it.
4. **High availability and fault tolerance:** Distributed Databases attain high availability and fault tolerance by spreading their data

across multiple nodes. The system enables critical applications to operate without interruptions because it continues to function even when certain nodes become unavailable. This database architecture serves as the foundation for backup systems and disaster recovery solutions.

5. **Real-time data processing:** Database systems which operate across multiple locations allow organizations to recover from disasters while supporting their real-time data processing needs. Data processing and analysis must take place here as it's generated. The system uses distributed databases to divide its workload across multiple machines which permits the operation of Internet of Things systems, real-time analytics, and data streaming platforms.

2.2.2 Distributed Database Features

Distributed databases use various technologies and techniques to enhance database performance and operational efficiency while maintaining database security and simplifying complex processes. The following technologies and techniques work together to achieve this goal:

- **Data distribution.** The IT teams need to determine the locations for data fragments and replicas throughout the distributed database system. The data allocation strategy selects storage locations based on three factors which include actual node positions and data access patterns and network infrastructure design. The proper allocation method improves system performance by reducing both network delays and data transmission duration. The system assigns frequently accessed data storage to end-user proximity nodes while allocating less commonly used data storage to remote nodes. The data distribution technology known as sharing enables distributed databases to divide their data into smaller pieces which they distribute across multiple network nodes.
- **Data replication.** With replication of data, a distributed database creates multiple copies of data and stores the copies on different nodes. The system achieves increased fault tolerance and data availability because users can access data from alternate nodes when one node fails. Users experience improved read performance because they can access data from the closest or least busy node. The challenge with data replication requires organizations to ensure all

data replicas maintain their data consistency.

- **Data transparency.** Even though the database is distributed, users and applications should be able to interact with it as if it were a single, unified system. The database management system (DBMS) achieves data transparency by managing all tasks related to data distribution and storage, which allows users to see the complete and consistent view of all data.
- **Centralized administration.** The complex structures of distributed database systems need their central administration system which enables administrators to control and observe system operations as a unified entity. The central interface allows administrators to perform system setup and configuration tasks while they can scale nodes between different sizes and conduct backup operations and monitoring tasks and security configuration and performance testing and multiple additional activities.
- **Authorization.** Authorization means granting or denying access to system resources or data based on user roles and permissions. The system provides access through two methods which include using lists of authorized personnel and using role-based access control (RBAC) systems as the more common method.
- **Identity management.** Identity management encompasses all business procedures in addition to technology which enable organizations to control digital identities for their authentication needs. The field of identity management controls three main components, which include user credentials and identity verification and user authentication.
- **Fault tolerance.** Fault tolerance is one of the core reasons to maintain a distributed database. The system's capacity to function properly even in the case of a hardware or software malfunction. When a node within the distributed system fails, the database can automatically switch to a backup node to maintain continuous service.
- **Data locality controls.** This is simply placing data in servers that are closer to the users or applications that need that data most. The goal is to reduce network latency and improve performance, so data fragments and replicas are stored to optimize for geographic location, network topology, and access patterns. In addition, data locality controls are often used to help comply with data sovereignty regulations.

- **Security architecture.** This is a combination of measures taken at the server, network, and software layers to protect a distributed database against breaches, illegal entry, and additional security risks. These precautions can include strong control mechanisms to stop unwanted access, secure communication protocols, and encryption of data both in transit and at rest.

2.2.3 Types of Distributed Databases

A distributed database can take many different forms. The best option for an organization depends on its primary use case. The forms a distributed database can take include the following:

- **Homogenous.** This refers to a distributed database in which all nodes in the network use the same database and "database management system" (DBMS) and share the same data structure.
- **Heterogenous.** Here, the nodes in the network might use different database management systems and have different data structures that require an application to translate and integrate data from various systems. A heterogeneous database system can result from adding new functionality to a legacy database or quickly integrating different systems, as when one organization acquires another.
- **Federated.** A federated database allows multiple databases to work together as a single database. Each database maintains its autonomy but can share data and cooperate with all databases in the federated system.
- **Partitioned.** In a partitioned database, Partitions are smaller, easier-to-manage sections of data that are kept on a different node in the network.
- **Hybrid.** Federated and partitioned components are combined in a hybrid distributed database. It can include both autonomous databases that cooperate and partitioned data that is distributed across nodes.
- **Replicated.** To provide high availability and fault tolerance, copies of the data are kept on several nodes in a replicated database. To maintain consistency, changes to data are immediately propagated to backup replicas.

2.2.4 Advantages of Distributed Databases

Today's always-on, data-intensive world is characterized by increasing demands on an organization's data management system. Distributed databases are key to effectively using data to power applications, gain insights, and remain competitive in the digital age.

Specific advantages of distributed database systems include the following:

- **Availability.** By replicating data, A distributed database system can enhance performance across several nodes data accessibility—even if nodes fail. Another common technique, called load balancing, distributes queries or transactional workloads across multiple nodes to maintain responsiveness even during peak usage.
- **Cost-effectiveness.** Distributed databases are a great way to get the most out of commodity hardware and cloud services. monolithic database solutions. These systems can be less expensive than conventional ones since they distribute data among several nodes and scale automatically as necessary.
- **Flexibility.** The modular nature of distributed databases allows administrators, or automated systems, to add and remove nodes without disrupting the entire system. Organizations have the ability to customize their distributed databases according to their particular needs through this flexible system, which allows them to choose from various data models and storage methods and deployment options.
- **Performance.** There are several ways a distributed database can improve performance. The system uses sharing and replication and locality controls as its performance-enhancing techniques. The system achieves better query performance through its data partitioning system which distributes manageable data chunks across multiple nodes. Through data replication and locality controls administrators can store data closer to frequent users which results in faster response times.
- **Reliability.** Distributed database architectures achieve enhanced system reliability through their ability to replicate data and their built-in fault tolerance capabilities. The system creates multiple data copies which it stores on different nodes through its data replication feature. The system will automatically switch to another node when

one node experiences a failure which enables the system to keep running.

- **Scalability.** A distributed database system enables capacity adjustments through its ability to change system size according to user traffic and data storage requirements. The system achieves growth capacity through network node expansion, while cloud services enable automatic reduction of nodes to optimize infrastructure expenses.

2.2.5 Applications of Distributed Database

Organizations choose to run distributed databases for many reasons. The primary advantage of the system enables automatic distribution of high workload demands which includes both transactional and analytical work across different system instances to prevent any single server from becoming a performance constraint. The systems provide organizations with multiple solutions to achieve their various operational needs and solve their different organizational challenges.

- **Global data distribution.** A distributed database system becomes necessary when an application needs to function across multiple countries throughout the world. The system uses this capability to keep data nearby users which results in faster access times for both reading and writing operations. The system performance delivery of real-time applications to users enhances their experience. The system needs to establish multiple methods for achieving resilience. If a data center or server in one region experiences an outage, users in other regions can still access the data and the application itself from local operational nodes.
- **Efficient scaling**. Distributed databases allow for quick, horizontal scaling by allowing administrators to add more nodes to the system in response to increased data volume, more complex requests, and more concurrent users. This scaling can also be set up to happen autonomously.
- **Data locality and compliance.** For organizations with stringent data governance rules or regional data residency requirements, distributed databases allow administrators to store data in the geographic location where it's generated, enabling these companies to comply with local mandates.

- **High availability and fault tolerance.** A distributed database is vital for mission-critical workloads because, Data is kept accessible even in the event that some nodes fail by being replicated across other nodes. Most disaster recovery architectures are based on a distributed database model—following a catastrophic event, data can be quickly recovered from a distant node or region.
- **Performance.** With its data and workloads distributed a database system can enhance performance across several servers by lowering the load on any single node. This can lead to faster query responses and better overall system performance.

2.2.6 Examples of Distributed Databases

The distributed database model excels in providing increased processing power through horizontal scalability, data locality, and fault tolerance. The specific database an organization chooses, however, will often come down to the needs and limitations of the company's applications. Some use cases require the absolute consistency of an ACID-compliant relational database, while others are better suited to a BASE-type database that offers eventual consistency. Let's look at some examples of each

Examples of ACID-compliant systems include:

- **Oracle Database.** Oracle Database facilitates globally distributed, linearly scalable, multimodal databases that support structured and unstructured data. Through unique multicloud agreements with Microsoft Azure, AWS, and Google Cloud, Oracle's distributed database service runs in these hyperscalers' data centers to unify management and operations and help eliminate network latency and the cost of moving data across clouds.
- **Google Cloud Spanner.** Using Cloud Spanner, a globally distributed database service offered by Google Cloud, is horizontally scalable. The service provides automatic sharding, global distribution, and strong consistency.
- **CockroachDB.** This distributed SQL database features ACID transactions, distributed architecture, and multiregion deployments.
- **YugabyteDB.** YugabyteDB is an open-source distributed SQL database that blends the scalability and resilience of NoSQL databases with relational database functionality.

Examples of BASE-type systems include:

- **Oracle Database.** Oracle's multimodal Using the JSON data model, the database facilitates the building of schema less applications. This enables a hybrid development strategy that combines the advantages of an enterprise-class relational database with the application development of NoSQL document storage.
- **Apache Cassandra.** A distributed NoSQL database called Cassandra was created to manage massive volumes of data across commodity machines. It offers good accessibility at a minimal cost.
- **Couchbase.** A distributed NoSQL database, Couchbase features document-oriented storage, in-memory caching, and automatic sharding, as well as multi-data center replication.
- **MongoDB.** A well-known NoSQL database with a document-oriented data model is MongoDB. High performance, simple scalability, and features are its main goals flexible schemas, automatic sharding, and replica sets for high availability.
- **Redis.** This NoSQL data stores that are in-memory can serve as message brokers, databases, and/or caches. Strings, hashes, lists, and sets are just a few of the many data structures it supports. In its enterprise offering, Redis attempts to offer both BASE- and ACID-compliant systems.

2.2.7 Challenges of Distributed Databases

While sharding and distributed databases offer Although there are substantial advantages in terms of availability, scalability, and performance, there are also related difficulties. During the design and implementation, these must be carefully taken into account phases.

- **Complexity.** Managing the many physical or virtual servers in Managing a single centralized database is easier than managing a distributed database. Sophisticated algorithms and protocols are required to handle data distribution, replication, and consistency. Cloud providers now offer fully managed databases to help more organizations take advantage of distributed database architectures.
- **Data consistency.** It can be difficult to guarantee that all data copies are consistent throughout the network of servers that comprise a distributed database, particularly in the case of node crashes or

network outages. In an ACID-compliant database, data consistency can be tightly maintained; in a BASE-type database, which may be more economical for large-scale web applications, data constancy can be eventually consistent.

- **Network delays (latency).** Time delays, or latency, in communication between nodes in a distributed database can be caused by the quantity of switches and routers connecting them. The system's overall performance may be impacted by excessive latency, especially for transactions that call for instantaneous consistency.
- **Security risks.** Because distributed databases have more access points and a more complicated network, they may be more susceptible to security risks.

2.3 Relational vs NoSQL Databases in the Cloud

Databases are essential for organizing, storing, and retrieving data. The two major types of databases are the both non-relational (NoSQL) and relational (SQL). The database type selection is crucial to the development of efficient and moving systems since both can offer different features and benefits.

A relational database, sometimes referred to as a SQL database is a kind of database that organizes data into tables made up of columns of attributes or properties and rows of unique records. These tables are linked together using primary and foreign keys. A foreign key is a column in one table that points to the primary key in another table; there will be a relationship between the two databases. In contrast, a primary key is a unique identifier of a record in a database.

Tables can be linked to one another using main and foreign keys. Indicatively, a customer ID primary key in the customer table and a customer ID foreign key in the order table can be used to link the two tables. Because it is simple to obtain information from various tables, relational databases are perfect for managing complicated data.

Relational databases can have a vast number of applications in both small and large enterprise-level systems. They are really well-liked due to the ability to readily adjust to the altering demands and the capability to process diverse types of data.

Because they can manage unstructured or NoSQL databases are non-relational databases that store semi-structured data, are growing in popularity information. Since a regular relational database is a pre-defined structure in which one tries to organize and manage data, then it may not be easy to store and analyze such type of data.

The term "unstructured data" refers to information that is not in line with any specific data model or schema. Examples of such data include the social media posts and other data created by human beings and may be challenging to handle with a conventional SQL query. Conversely, semi-structured data is slightly structured and is not bound to a rigid pattern. Semi structured data include machine logs and sensor data.

Unstructured and semi-structured data can be handled by non-relational databases. Data can be altered without requiring the creation of a schema because it is not restricted to a set schema. Rather, they employ a range of data models to satisfy a set of data forms and types. They are thus suitable to handle large, complex data that may evolve as time goes.

2.3.1 Types of Non-Relational Databases

The non-relational database types—graph, document, columnar, and key-value databases—will be covered in this section. We will discuss the characteristics, advantages, and uses of non-relational databases to assist you in selecting the one that could best suit your particular requirements.

- **Graph Databases**

A database with graphs Graphs are used to store and display data in this kind of database. It works best when searching for and assessing intricate data linkages. Data is represented by the nodes (vertices) and edges in a graph database. Organizations or concepts in the form of people, places and objects are the entities that are depicted by nodes whereas their relationships are depicted by edges. In a social network, such as one node would represent one individual, an edge connecting two people's nodes would symbolize their friendship.

Every node and edge may have some features that characterize their traits and qualities. For instance, the edge, which signifies friendship, can have such a property as date when the connection was established, whereas the human node can have such properties as name, age, and location.

The graph databases are useful in situations like recommendation engines, social networks, and fraud detection systems where links between the data components are imperative.

- **Document Databases**

One kind of non-SQL Document databases are those that store and retrieve data as documents. A single document may have arrays and hierarchical data structures since it is a single record or object its schema may change over time, they are incredibly versatile and scalable.

Because Document databases are ideal for use with modern online applications that handle a variety of data types since they are designed to handle unstructured or semi-structured data. They offer indexing and aggregation and use document-based formats like JSON or BSON.

In addition to being able to handle complex queries and large data volumes, document databases make it simple to add or remove fields and documents without the need for a schema. The document databases may also be implemented in multiple servers to provide better performance and can be easily scaled.

- **Columnar Databases**

A database is a columnar database in which data are stored and accessed by column, as opposed to storing and accessing data by row. A columnar database contains values in each row, and these values are of all the columns which correspond to different characteristics or properties of the data.

Suppose that you have a large dataset, such as a customer database of an online store, which has millions of rows and several columns. The columns may contain features such as the name of the customer, their address, date of birth and previous purchases that the customer has made.

All the columns in the columnar database are stored separately. It implies that you only need to read the columns that contain the attributes you are interested in when you query the database to obtain customer data.

2.3.2 When To Use Relational vs. Non-Relational Databases

The data type, volume and elaborateness, and what you need the data to do is also one of the factors that will dictate whether you use either a non-relational database or a relational database.

Relational databases are a great choice when you must ensure the data is consistent, enable complex queries and have clear data schema. They are configured to process complex SQL statements with many tables and joins, enable transactions to maintain data consistency and store structured information which is described by a specific schema.

When managing enormous volumes of semi-structured or unstructured data and needing to enable fast throughput and low latency, non-relational databases are an excellent option. They are optimized for quick read and write performance, can grow horizontally to accommodate massive volumes of data, and are made to store data that does not follow a set structure.

Relational databases:

- E.g. online store that must handle and retain transactional data, including orders, payments, and inventories.
- A banking system or any other financial application, which requires high data integrity and consistency.
- Enterprise program, like a CRM or ERP system which requires complex structured data querying and analysis.

Non-relational databases:

- A social media network is required to store and retrieve user-generated content, including likes, comments, and postings.
- Recommendation engines and fraud detection systems are examples of real-time analytics applications that need quick and effective access to data.

- In order to meet the demand for a substantial amount of unstructured content, including images, videos, and audio files.

2.3.3 Features of Relational (SQL) Databases

Social folders have been popularly utilized in managing and storing data due to a variety of significant qualities. We shall discuss this in more detail below.

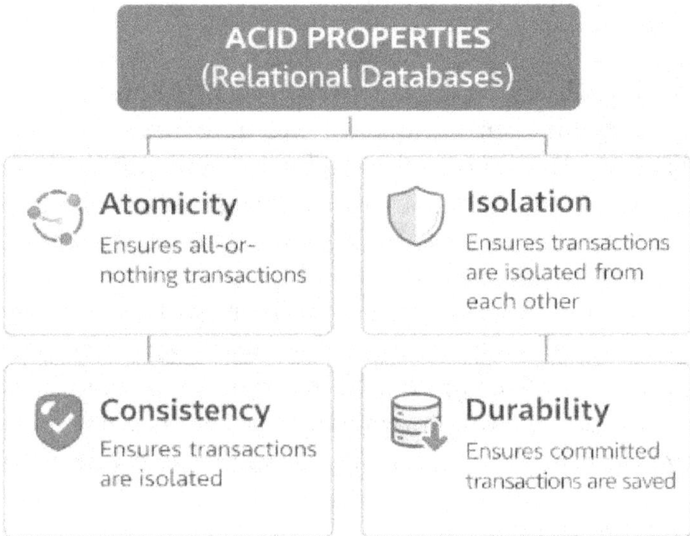

Figure 2.1: Features of Relational (SQL) Databases

1. **Atomicity:** Atomicity enables a transaction to be seen as a single, indivisible work unit. This implies that the transaction should either be completed completely or not. Any failure of any part of a transaction will roll-back the transaction to its original value.
2. **Consistency:** consistency ensures that the database is at all times in the proper state. It means that any changes that occur in the database must be based on some predefense rules or restrictions.
3. **Isolation:** It is possible to execute numerous transactions at the same time without affecting each other due to isolation. This means that although there are numerous transactions that might be in progress

at any given time, all the transactions would view the database as the one that is in contact with the database.

4. **Durability:** When a transaction is committed to the database, the property of durability ensures that the transaction will remain in the system indefinitely regardless of the system malfunction or other disturbance.

2.3.4 Pros and Cons of Relational (SQL) Databases

There are relational databases have a number of benefits and drawbacks. A some of the notable advantages and limitations of the use of relational databases are the following:

Pros:

Data consistency: Relational databases store and process data in an organization, thus providing data accuracy and consistency.

- **Scaling:** SQL databases can be useful in various applications since they can allow complex searches and analysis of large data sets.
- **Security:** SQL databases have several To safeguard private information and prevent unwanted access, security mechanisms like user authentication and access controls are used.
- **Excellent data integrity:** Relational databases assist in ensuring that data is accurate and consistent across time similar to the manner of strict guidelines and restrictions on data entry.

Cons:

- **Complexity:** The setup and management of relational database may be complicated and demand a particular expertise.
- **Cost:** Implementing and maintaining relational databases can be costly, especially in large-scale applications.
- **Low scalability:** The relational databases could not be suitable in case of very large or dynamically changing datasets, though they can be scaled significantly.
- **Performance:** Relational databases might not be as fast as other database forms when it comes to making large number of transactions or complex queries.

2.3.5 Features of Non-Relational (NoSQL) Databases

Large volumes of unstructured or semi-structured data can be processed using non-relational databases. Below, we will go into further depth about this.

Figure 2.2: Features of Non-Relational (NoSQL) Databases

1. **NoSQL:** NoSQL Databases lack a predetermined schema or organization and are, therefore, schemeless. Information may be stored in many different forms.
2. **High scalability:** NoSQL databases have great performance capabilities, it because of its highly scalable design, can manage heavy traffic loads and massive data volumes. To guarantee quick reaction times even with massive volumes of data, they employ distributed processing and caching.

3. **Scalability:** Additionally, NoSQL databases can effortlessly manage massive amounts of data because they can expand with additional servers to the database cluster due to their horizontal scaling.
4. **Scalable data modelling:** NoSQL databases can have a flexible data model, which is able to handle unstructured, semi-structured, and structured data.
5. **Fault tolerance and availability:** NoSQL databases are built with high availability and fault tolerance in mind. To guarantee that the data is accessible even in the event that one or more servers fail, they employ sharding and replication.
6. **Open source:** Since many NoSQL databases are available as open source, it follows that developers can modify and enhance their source code freely.

2.3.6 Pros and Cons of Non-Relational (NoSQL) Databases

There are a few benefits and drawbacks of non-relational databases. The primary advantages and disadvantages of using a non-relational database are enumerated as under.

Pros:

- **Flexibility:** Because they can handle unstructured or semi-structured data, non-relational databases are perfect for large data environments and modern web applications.
- **Scalability**: Non-relational databases can handle large amounts of data and high read and write traffic since they are designed to be incredibly scalable.
- **Performance:** When managing intricate queries and substantial volumes of data, non-relational databases can offer excellent performance.
- **Distributed architecture:** By distributing non-relational databases over several servers, performance can be enhanced and horizontal scaling made simple.
- **Agile development:** The non-relational data structures are suitable in agile development model since they enable Fields and documents can be easily added or removed without altering procedures.

- **Economical**: For large-scale applications, non-relational databases may be more economical than regular databases.

Cons:

- **Limited query support:** Relational databases provide more query support than NoSQL databases. Complex enquiries and data analysis may become more challenging as a result.
- **Absence of standardization:** There is no common query language for NoSQL databases as compared to SQL, and this may complicate the creation and maintenance of applications that use these databases.
- **Consistency**: To achieve high performance and scalability, the NoSQL databases can forfeit consistency. This implies that data is not always precise and current.
- **Learning curve:** Because NoSQL systems employ different data models and APIs than conventional databases, developers accustomed to working with SQL-based databases may encounter a learning curve. More time in training and development might be required to be competent in this.
- **Limited tooling:** Compared to relational databases, NoSQL databases could have less community support and tooling because they are still relatively new.
- **Data security:** NoSQL databases may not be as encrypted and controlled as relational databases.

2.4 Security and Compliance in Cloud Databases

A collection of security techniques known as "cloud security" were created to safeguard data, apps, and cloud infrastructure. These protections preserve data privacy by ensuring user and device authentication, data and resource access control, and data access control. They also help to guarantee data compliance norms.

Cloud database security basically protects the data of an organization against virus and data, distributed denial of service (DDoS) assaults, and hackers breach, unauthorised user access or utilization in cloud systems.

Cloud security has become quite important since the majority of firms are now implementing cloud computing in one way or another.

IT workers are still reluctant to transfer more apps and data to the cloud as a result of governance, regulatory, and security concerns. They worry that particularly private information and intellectual property could be harmed by more sophisticated cyberattacks or unintentional breaches.

To address this problem, corporate content and data protection are important components of cloud security. Maintaining your customers' trust and avoiding data theft and leaks is essential to safeguarding the resources that provide you a a competitive edge. For any business going to the cloud, like Google cloud storage, the ability of cloud database security to safeguard your massive data store and support is essential.

2.4.1 Cloud Database Security Issues

Cloud database systems are vulnerable to many of the same risks that affect cloud technologies. However, because of the massive volumes Considering potentially sensitive data kept in databases and the lack of security measures, the consequences could be disastrous if disregarded.

These problems and difficulties with network security provide network managers with an understanding of the types of hazards they may face when companies implement large cloud database storage systems, even though they are not comprehensive.

1. Data Breaches

Data breaches are perhaps the most frequent risk to cloud databases, according to media reports. In a data breach, hackers obtain unauthorised access to confidential data stored in a cloud environment and use it for their own benefit. As more information is stored online in one place, data breaches are surely becoming more catastrophic, potentially impacting millions of employees or clients at once.

2. Account Hijacking

Hackers attempt to take control (or hijack) a user's account by using phishing tactics or software security weaknesses.

When a hacker obtains a user's login credentials, they typically change the password, preventing the user from taking control of their accounts and jeopardizing identity and access control in general. You can access any files or other anything stored in the user's cloud using this option, including database data that concurrently contains information about several users.

3. Data Loss

Another plausible result of an attacker gaining access to private data is that the intruder will delete it in order to cause the owner inconvenience. Users risk losing their files forever if they don't keep current backups in case something or someone manipulates them. When every file is stored on a single cloud-based server, deletions may propagate to every user device, causing all of the files to be deleted at once.

2.4.2 Cloud Database Security Best Practices

Here are some recommended techniques for cloud database security to address the aforementioned problems:

- **Recognize Your Model of Shared Responsibility**

Any security problems in a private data center are the organization's responsibility. IT security, however, is the public cloud's responsibility. A shared responsibility paradigm is the name given to this legal requirement.

Businesses should examine the company's shared security responsibility policies and decide who is in charge of what components of cloud security before choosing a cloud vendor. Misunderstandings and misinterpretations may be avoided thanks to this function. Furthermore, having a clear understanding of roles can assist prevent security mishaps caused by certain security requirements becoming overlooked.

- **Inquire Specifically About Security with Your Cloud Provider**

Businesses should ask their public cloud providers about the security procedures and techniques in addition to outlining shared responsibilities. Although it is Although it is simple to believe that the largest corporations are in charge of their security, different vendors may have very different security protocols. In particular, if the system offers role-based access, you should enquire about identity and access management.

- **Create and Implement Cloud Security Policies**

Written policies outlining who can use cloud services, how to use them, and what data can be stored there should be in place for every business. They must also outline the specific security measures that staff members must take to safeguard cloud-hosted data and applications.

To ensure that everyone is following the rules, security staff should preferably have automated mechanisms in place. The cloud vendor's policy enforcement feature might be sufficient in some situations to meet the needs of the business.

2.4.3 The challenges of cloud data security

- **Greater visibility**

Robust cloud computing allows you to monitor your cloud's internal operations, including what data assets you have and where they are located, who is using your cloud services, and what kind of data they are accessing data protection procedures.

- **Easy backups and recovery**

Your teams won't have to keep an eye on manual backups or troubleshoot issues thanks to cloud data security's many features and solutions for automating and standardizing backups. You can also restore and recover data and apps in minutes using cloud-based disaster recovery.

- **Cloud data compliance**

Strong cloud data security systems are made to comply with regulations, which include understanding where data is kept, who can access it, how it is processed, and how it is safeguarded. To lower the likelihood of violations, cloud data loss prevention (DLP) makes it simple to find, categorize, and de-identify sensitive data.

- **Data encryption**

Organisations must safeguard sensitive data everywhere and at all times. Cloud service providers help you with secure cloud data transmission, storage, and sharing by employing multiple levels of advanced encryption to protect cloud data both in transit and at rest.

- **Lower costs**

The administrative and managerial burden related to cloud data security is decreased, as is the total cost of ownership (TCO). Additionally, cloud providers deliver the most recent security features and technologies, which simplify the work of security professionals through automation, faster integration, and ongoing alerts.

- **Advanced incident detection and response**

One benefit of cloud data security is that providers make investments in state-of-the-art AI technologies and integrated security analytics, which enable you to quickly identify and handle security events by automatically looking for questionable activity.

2.5 Scalability and High Availability in Cloud Systems

The ability of a system to continue functioning and being available even in the event that some of its components fail is referred to as high availability (HA). Uptime percentages are frequently used to quantify it, with the goal of reaching "nines" in terms of availability. As an example, five nines or 99.999 percent uptime will equivalent to about five minutes of lost time annually. For cloud-based systems, where minor malfunctions can impact significant repercussions, this (high) level of uptime is essential. Investment and strategy preparation are required to achieve this degree of availability.

The gold standard is five-nine uptime but there are several unavoidable hurdles that make it practically impossible to achieve 100 percent high availability. In cloud computing, it is imperative to endeavor to achieve the best uptime rates in the setting of HA through the use of a number of strategies such as redundancy and failover.

2.5.1 The Challenges in Maintaining High Availability

High accessibility is not an easy undertaking as not only a number of issues may disrupt system uptime but also the unexpected traffic overflow or hardware failures. These challenges need to be identified and mitigated to ensure that it does not compromise the dependability of its services at all times.

1. **Hardware Failures:** Hardware failures are also unexpected failures that may happen even in the most advanced hardware. Poor hardware issue mitigation, e.g. server crashes, malfunctioning of the storage system or network outages, may lead to downtime. Redundancy is absolutely necessary because cloud platforms are especially susceptible to such problems in hardware.
2. **Software Bugs:** Software may also cause disruptions, such as bugs or inaccurate settings. To remain available, it is important to identify and fix issues in time.
3. **Traffic surges** may overwhelm your system (either caused by ill-intentioned individuals like in DDoS attacks) or by legitimate users. The availability of your system can be compromised unless it has been made to scale.
4. **Architecture bottlenecks:** Bottlenecks in the hardware or software of a system may seriously impair its capability to switch traffic or to rapidly recover following any error.

These tasks show the need to reduce strategies such as proactive scaling, redundancy, and failover strategies in maintaining high availability.

2.5.2 Building Blocks of High Availability: Ensuring Seamless Uptime in Critical Systems

Ensuring that systems are running 24 hours a day is not merely a luxury anymore in the globalized world, but an essential requirement. High availability is the basis of modern infrastructure and ensures that there is continuity of services even when there are component failures. Nevertheless, ensuring high availability is best achieved through proper integration of key building aspects that ensure resilience and not through the incorporation of the latest technology.

However, it may take time and effort to differentiate technical enablers and building blocks. Building blocks are the basic elements that maintain system availability, i.e. redundancy, monitoring and failover. Technical enablers, in their turn, are platforms or tools like automation frameworks or cloud services that effectively provide and use these building blocks. In order to comprehend their role in the high-availability environment, we should take these basic elements apart.

1. Redundancy

Redundancy is the foundation of high availability. This fundamental component guarantees that there is an easy replacement of another component in case of failure. The concept of redundancy operates in a number of levels:

- **Hardware Redundancy:** This will prevent a single point of failure by means of duplicate servers, storage or networking hardware.
- **Software Redundancy:** Cloud systems like AWS and Azure contain software to redirect traffic If a major system fails to backup systems.
- **Data Center Redundancy:** With the distributed services of multiple data centers, you can be rest assured that there will be a capable replacement of a given data center, in case it collapses.

To ensure smooth availability, redundancy schemes such as active-passive schemes, where the backup is activated only in case of a malfunction of the primary system, and active-active schemes, where numerous systems serve the traffic simultaneously should be used.

2. Failure Detection and Monitoring

The next ingredient is active surveillance. Monitoring technologies will prevent the emergence of small errors into great failures since they can detect potential issues at their initial stages. Such systems offer real time information that enables immediate action as parameters of health such as CPU utilization, memory and disc I/O are constantly being monitored. To guarantee that every component operates at maximum efficiency, A range of monitoring services are provided by third-party companies and cloud providers options. In the event that one of the servers starts to malfunction, the automatic failover procedures make sure that a failure is prevented before it even turns into a whole outage.

3. Failover Mechanisms

It has high availability safety net. Failover methods redirect the workloads to backup systems when there is a failure of a component. These mechanisms are of two major categories:

- Automatic Failover: This system reduces the downtime and switches to backup automatically without the assistance of a human.
- Failover by hand Here, there should be some human intervention and this may lead to an extended outage.

During practical cases, it is very important that failover solutions are put to test on a regular basis to make sure things function properly in real-world situations. Businesses can employ automated failover solutions from cloud service providers such as Google Cloud, AWS, and Azure to maintain their services.

By concentrating on these essential construction elements, organizations' high availability is guaranteed. Tools for monitoring, cloud services, and automated failover are examples of technology enablers components applied by them. An awareness of this difference is needed in order to build a strong, 24/7 infrastructure.

2.5.3 High Availability: Technical Enablers for Cloud-Based Applications

It is essential to put the relevant technical enablers that ensure high availability to ensure companies do not lose millions of dollars due to downtime. Now we shall continue more into the details of what they are and how they safeguard against disruptions.

1. Data Backup and Recovery

One of the core principles of high availability is data backup and recovery. Frequent, automated backups are necessary to avoid the loss of data during the failures of the system. Besides the safety net, backups will also ensure that data could be restored in a short period in case of failure in case of outage to minimize the downtime.

Discussing procedures of data recovery, it is important to keep in mind that companies should be capable of restoring apps and data as fast as possible to get systems functioning once again. The rate of recovery may significantly affect the survival of a business.

Moreover, one of the elements of disaster recovery is the specification of a local or cloud-based backup. There is more resilience with cloud-based backups which store copies elsewhere compared to local backups which have shorter restoration time. This enhances the overall high availability posture of enterprises by assuring them that they are able to recover their data at a distant place in the event of disastrous hardware failure or natural calamities.

2. Load Balancing

Another essential component of high availability is loading balancing, which makes sure that incoming traffic is split equally among several servers or instances. By doing this, load balancers can guarantee maximum performance when there is a traffic spike, as well as ensure that individual servers are not overloaded.

Businesses can use a range of load-balancing strategies, each appropriate for specific application needs. For example, least connections routes traffic to the server with the fewest active connections while round-robin distributes it in a sequential manner. By preventing bottlenecks, these methods guarantee smooth application availability throughout dispersed systems. Effective workload distribution and resilience can be achieved by using suitable load-balancing technologies.

Geographically dispersed load balancers are crucial for companies that operate across multiple locations. These systems lower latency and enhance performance for consumers all across the world by using data center proximity to route traffic. Furthermore, in the event that one region goes offline, this global diversification ensures that traffic may be rerouted to another, preserving high availability despite regional malfunctions.

3. Clustering

By offering redundancy and failover capabilities, clustering ensures that other nodes may keep handling the burden in the cluster in the event of a node failure. In high-availability systems, this node-level redundancy is essential to ensuring continuous service.

It is essential to comprehend the concept of cluster quorum in a clustering configuration. In addition to preventing split-brain situations, which occur when several system components act independently, the quorum aids in maintaining data consistency. This consistency guarantees that even in the event of partial failures, the system will continue to function properly.

By guaranteeing in the event of a failure, synchronous clustering minimizes data loss by real-time data replication among nodes. For systems that prioritize throughput above instantaneous data consistency, asynchronous clustering is a superior option., nevertheless, since this can add latency. The trade-offs of synchronous and asynchronous clustering, which weigh performance against data loss risk, are contingent upon the particular requirements of the application.

4. Scalability and Capacity Management

The capacity to scale out (horizontally) or up (vertically) becomes an essential part of high availability as cloud systems expand. While scaling out is adding new servers to meet rising demand, scaling up entails boosting an existing server's resources (such as CPU or RAM). Both strategies assist in handling increased traffic volumes, guaranteeing that systems continue to function even as demand rises.

By dynamically modifying resources in response to real-time traffic and load, auto-scaling systems go beyond scalability. Businesses may make sure They have the means to autonomously scale up or down in order to handle traffic spikes without the need for human intervention.

Cloud bursting, in which on-premise systems briefly move to the cloud to manage peak demand, is a related idea. Because it allows them to leverage the cloud's capacity during peak hours without having to permanently move all workloads, this strategy is especially helpful for businesses with hybrid infrastructures. Cloud bursting provides adaptability, assisting companies in controlling expenses while guaranteeing they have the resources required to sustain high availability at crucial times.

Lastly, by automating container deployment, scaling, and operation, solutions like container orchestration systems (like Kubernetes) aid in managing scalability in cloud environments. These platforms make it simple for companies to scale their applications, which enhances resource efficiency and guarantees high availability as the system expands.

2.5.4 Design Principles for High Availability in the Cloud

High accessibility in cloud computing is vital in a way that in case of failures, the apps and systems do not come to a halt with minimal downtime.

To achieve a high availability in the cloud, a coordinated approach that incorporates a number of design principles and technical facilitators is required to ensure that critical services are always available. This is a summary of the key design concepts to consider.

1. Eradication of Single points of failure

Designing high availability is an important element of removing single points of failure. Any component of a system that will result in a single point of failure a complete failure of that system in case of a failure. These are severe threats to the availability of the systems and it may be at the hardware level, software level or network level.

This is minimized by redundancy and load balancing. Redundancy ensures that the backup is ready to perform the tasks of the other component that fails. Server replication across multiple availability zones, such as that, contributes to the elimination of single points of failure in the cloud infrastructure. Similarly, load balancing is used to make sure that no server is overloaded by allocating the traffic between multiple servers or instances.

2. Carrying out Load balancing and Clustering

Load balancing equalizes incoming requests to ensure that servers do not overload which is an essential aspect of high availability. Other load balancing techniques including least connections and round-robin are used to effectively allocate the demand among servers to ensure peak availability and performance. Learn more about how the scalability, availability and performance of this resource are improved through load balancing and clustering.

Cloud providers such as AWS and Azure are built with load balancers that actively reroute traffic according to performance and health of the separate servers. Clustering provides an extra level of redundancy because by connecting together servers (nodes) to act as one system, they perform. A cluster can also have requests that are processed continuously by the other remaining nodes in case of failure of one node. Another concept applied in clustering is quorum, which ensures that there is consistency in data and the system does not break down (split-brain situations) when there are failures in nodes. Combined with load balancing, clustering presents high failover which enhances the general accessibility of cloud-based software.

3. Data Replication for Redundancy

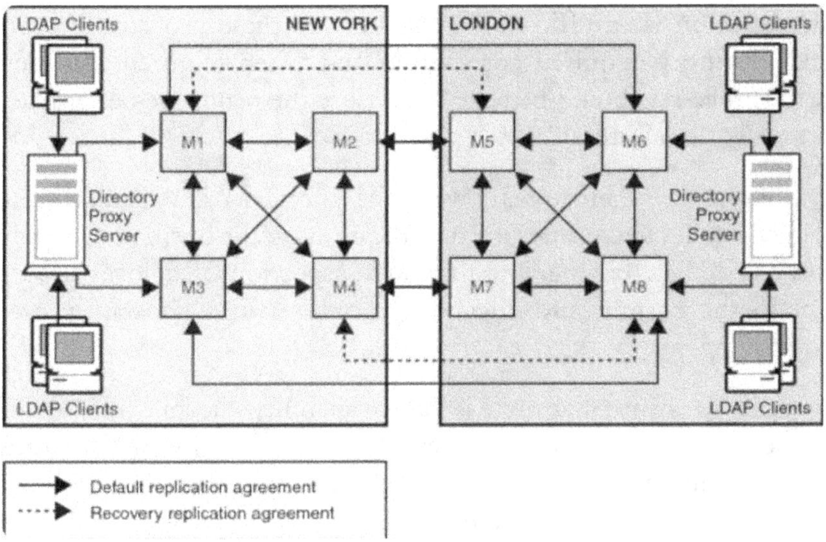

Figure 2.3: Data Replication

One of the strategies that can be used to achieve high availability is data replication which is used to ensure that data is replicated reliably over multiple locations. Replication of data to multiple availability zones or regions in cloud environments is used to protect against disaster and local outage losses of data. Such redundancy will ensure that the system can still be used with the help of data copied elsewhere in case one geographical area has an issue.

Replication of data in geographically dispersed locations is among the best ways to guarantee that business is not affected once it becomes stagnant and that the data is not lost.

4. Record keeping, Testing, and validating Failover and Failback Processes

In order to ensure that there is high availability, the failover and failback processes should be documented, tested, and verified alongside redundancy and load balancing. Whereas failback is applying services back to the main system after it has been reinstated, failover is removing single points of failure. Any component of a system that will result in a single point of failure

Detailed documentation ensures that, the teams can reduce downtime in case of failure, by observing the laid down procedures. Yet, lack of documentation is insufficient. To make sure these procedures function, regular testing is required correctly as and when required. Failover and failback processes should be tested to ensure the teams are better placed to face real-world failures.

Moreover, these processes have to be checked on a regular basis and updated in order to consider the modifications to the business requirements or system design. Frequent testing and inspection of failover procedures maintain the current and effective procedures in a constantly evolving environment.

In order to ensure that there is high availability, the failover and failback processes should be documented, tested, and verified alongside redundancy and load balancing. Whereas failback is applying services back to the main system after it has been reinstated, failover is switching to a holdup system in the event of a breakdown.

Detailed documentation ensures that, the teams can reduce downtime in case of failure, by observing the laid down procedures. Yet, lack of documentation is not enough. Regular testing is necessary to ensure that these processes work correctly as and when required. Failover and failback processes should be tested to ensure the teams are better placed to face real-world failures.

Moreover, these processes have to be checked on a regular basis and updated in order to consider the modifications to the business requirements or system design. In a setting that is continuously changing, routine testing and inspection of failover protocols preserve the current and efficient protocols.

2.5.5 Key Metrics for Measuring High Availability

Now we shall look at the main metrics that business apply to assess system availability and quantify high availability in order to prevent system failures and satisfy user expectations.

1. Uptime

Uptime, or the percentage of time a system is online, functional, and user-accessible, is the main measure of high availability. It can also be stated as a percentage, such as 99.9, 99.99, or 99.999, which denotes various annual permitted downtimes. A 99.9% uptime system, for example can be out of operation about 8.76 hours in a given year whereas a system that has 99.99% uptime will only allow 52.56 minutes.

The uptime is very important as it has a direct impact on the business continuity and user experience. In some cases, especially in such fields as e-commerce and financial services where businesses have to keep operating, downtime will lead not only to financial damages but also to dissatisfied consumers and a negative image of a business. To retain the trust of the customers, achieving the maximum uptime is critical to cloud services like those provided by Google Cloud, AWS, and Azure.

2. Service Level Agreement (SLAs)

The service providers and their clients have a contractual agreement in the form of SLAs that usually contain the expected uptime percentage. Such contracts make suppliers accountable besides setting expectations of the clients. An example is when cloud service providers such as Amazon Web Services (AWS) can promise some form of uptime (say 99.99) and refund customers when they fall short of it. These guarantees motivate the providers to establish the necessary infrastructure, monitoring and recovery plans to maintain their end of the bargain.

3. Recovery Time Objective (RTO) and Recovery Point Objective (RPO

- **RTO:** RTO specifies how long a system can go offline without seriously harming the company. To put it simply, it's the deadline for restoring a service following an outage.
- **RPO:** RPO, is, however, the maximum amount of data loss—measured in terms of time—that a business is willing to tolerate. It's shows how long it will take to retrieve data following an outage.

When establishing disaster recovery (DR) plans, these KPIs are essential for organizations. For example, if a severe failure occurs on an e-commerce platform, the RTO can be set to 30 minutes to ensure that While the RPO may be set to five minutes to guarantee that Data is restored five minutes prior to the outage, at the latest, the site is back online during that time.

Setting Expectations

Organizations can set reasonable expectations for internal teams and customers by defining RTO and RPO. By ensuring that the infrastructure required to achieve these recovery objectives is in place, this planning enables businesses to allocate resources efficiently. To reduce data loss and downtime a bank with minimal RTO and RPO standards, for instance, can make significant investments in automated failover systems and real-time data replication.

4. Mean Time Between Failures (MTBF) and Mean Time to Recovery (MTTR)

- **MTBF:** MTBF is a prediction metric that indicates how long a system is anticipated to function flawlessly. By indicating the rate of system failures, it aids organizations in evaluating the dependability of their systems.
- **MTTR:** This is the average time required to restart a failure, but it is calculated by MTTR. It includes detection, diagnosis, repair and mode of verification.

Understanding system resilience entails an understanding of MTBF as well as that of MTTR. Although a low MTTR is an indicator of a faster recovery process, which will guarantee less disruption to end users, a high MTBF is an indicator of a reliable system with minimal failure.

Improving Reliability

Infrastructure organisations can enhance MTBF by making investments in dependable and redundant hardware and software solutions, like the failover systems of Google Cloud or Elastic Load Balancing of AWS. When the automation of failure detection and recovery results in systems being able to go online faster, the MTTR is reduced. The collaboration with PayPal significantly reduced MTTR because it automatically detects and rectifies anomalies before turning into severe issues.

Multiple Choice Questions (MCQs)

1. **Which of the following best describes a cloud database?**
   A. A database stored only on a personal computer
   B. A database hosted and accessed through cloud infrastructure
   C. A database that does not require internet
   D. A spreadsheet stored in offline mode
2. **Which cloud database model stores data in rows and columns?**
   A. Key-value database
   B. Document database
   C. Relational database
   D. Graph database
3. **In distributed database architecture, data is mainly stored:**
   A. In only one central machine
   B. Across multiple interconnected nodes or locations
   C. Only in local storage devices
   D. In a paper-based system
4. **Which of the following is a major advantage of distributed database architecture?**
   A. Reduced fault tolerance
   B. Single point of failure
   C. Improved availability and performance
   D. No need for network connectivity
5. **Which type of cloud database is best suited for highly structured data and SQL queries?**
   A. NoSQL database
   B. Relational database
   C. Graph database only
   D. File storage system

6. Which of the following is a common feature of NoSQL databases?

A. Strict tabular schema only

B. Limited scalability

C. Flexible schema and horizontal scaling

D. Only supports SQL language

7. Which security practice helps protect cloud database data from unauthorized access?

A. Ignoring authentication

B. Data encryption

C. Public password sharing

D. Removing backups

8. In cloud databases, compliance refers to:

A. Increasing storage size only

B. Following legal, regulatory, and organizational standards

C. Reducing internet speed

D. Disabling access control

9. Scalability in cloud systems means:

A. The system can grow or shrink resources based on demand

B. The system can only work on one server

C. The system cannot handle increased users

D. The system removes all backups

10. High availability in cloud systems ensures that:

A. The system is frequently offline

B. The system remains accessible with minimal downtime

C. Only administrators can use the system

D. Data is deleted automatically

Answers

1	2	3	4	5	6	7	8	9	10
B	C	B	C	B	C	B	B	A	B

CHAPTER 3

BIG DATA TECHNOLOGIES AND FRAMEWORKS

3.1 FUNDAMENTALS OF BIG DATA PROCESSING

Large and varied datasets containing organized, semi-structured, and unstructured information are known as "big data." These datasets expand quickly and frequently beyond the processing and storage capacities of conventional data management solutions (Verma, 2022).

Because of advancements data is becoming increasingly available in digital technologies, such as artificial intelligence (AI), mobility, connection, and the Internet of Things (IoT). As data continues to grow and spread, new big data solutions are being developed to assist companies in gathering, analyzing, and comprehending data quickly enough to maximize its value.

"Big data" refers to enormous, varied datasets with enormous quantities that increase quickly over time. Machine learning, predictive modelling, and other advanced analytics leverage big data to solve business issues and make informed decisions (Ahmed et al., 2021).

An increasingly important organizational tool for analysis and decision-making is data. You can gain an awareness of the areas that impact your organization, such as customer purchasing patterns and market conditions, by using big data to uncover insights practices.

Businesses across all industries are being transformed by the following big data examples:

- Keeping an eye on consumer behaviour and purchase trends to offer highly tailored retail product recommendations for particular customers

- Keeping an eye on payment trends and comparing them to past customer behaviour to quickly identify fraud
- Combining hyperlocal traffic insights with data and information from each step of an order's shipment journey to assist fleet operators in optimizing last-mile delivery
- Analyzing unstructured medical data (such as research reports, clinical notes, and lab results) using AI-powered methods like natural language processing to gain fresh insights for improved patient care and treatment development
- Finding depressions and improving urban highway conservation using GPS, camera, and sensor image data
- Analyzing publicly accessible satellite pictures and geographic data to track, measure, visualize, and predict how supply chain activities affect society and the environment.

These illustrations demonstrate how companies employ big data technologies to support analytics, strategic decision-making, and operational effectiveness.

3.1.1 The Vs of Big Data

Big data will always be defined by volume, velocity, and diversity, even if definitions may differ slightly. These features of large data were initially outlined by Gartner in 2001 and are currently referred to as the "3 Vs of big data".

1. **Volume:** As the name implies, the most common characteristic of big data is its massive volume. This makes clear the massive volume of data that may be produced and gathered continually from many devices and sources.
2. **Velocity:** The speed at which data is produced is known as big data velocity. These days, data must be processed, retrieved, and analyzed at the same speed in order to have any significant impact because it is frequently generated in real time or very close to it.
3. **Variety:** There are numerous sources of organized, unstructured, or semi-structured data. These days, unstructured text, photos, audio, video files, or semi-structured forms like sensor data that cannot be arranged in a preset data schema are added to more conventional organized data (such data in spreadsheets or relational databases).

Three other Vs are value, variety, and veracity commonly mentioned when talking about using big data.

4. **Veracity:** Because big data is filthy, noisy, and prone to errors, controlling its quality and accuracy can be difficult. While larger datasets may be cumbersome and deceptive, smaller datasets may present an incomplete picture. The information dependability increases with its accuracy.
5. **Variability:** The constantly shifting interpretation of collected data might lead
6. **Value:** It's critical to assess the data's business worth. Big data must initially include the relevant information before it can generate insights that help direct decision-making properly analyzed.

3.1.2 Big data benefits

- **Better judgement:** Big data is necessary for an organization to become data-driven. When you are able to managing and analyzing your big data, you may identify patterns and acquire knowledge to improve your strategic and operational decisions.
- **Greater inventiveness and agility:** You may collect, to obtain a competitive advantage and make quick adjustments, utilizes big data to process and interpret real-time data points. These insights can direct and expedite the development, manufacturing, and introduction of new features, enhancements, and products.
- **Better customer experiences:** By merging and analysing both structured and unstructured data sources, you may learn more about customer knowledge, customisation, and ways to improve the experience to better meet the needs and expectations of customers.
- **Continuous intelligence:** By integrating big data allows you to continuously collect data, find new insights, and recognize new growth and value through automated, real-time data streaming and advanced data analytics opportunities.
- **More efficient operations:** By using big data analytics tools and capabilities, you can analyse data more quickly and obtain insights that can help you find areas where you can save costs, save time, and increase your overall productivity.
- **Improved risk management:** By making it easier to find, track, and provide large-scale data insights that improve control and mitigation analysis enhances risk assessment for enterprises methods.

3.1.3 Challenges of Implementing Big Data Analytics

Even though big data has several returns, businesses must be prepared for a number of obstacles while gathering, handling, and utilizing such massive amounts of data.

The large-scale data concerns that are most commonly brought up are as follows:

- **Data talent and skills shortage:** Big data is not a magic bullet, and until it is used in the hands of the correct individuals, its potential will be locked. The demand and shortage of data scientists, analysts, and engineers are high but they are few and therefore organizations may not utilize modern data technologies fully.
- **Speed of data growth:** Big data is growing exponentially, akin to the fact that it has a life of its own. It becomes difficult to cope with such a rapid increase without a powerful system of infrastructure that will allow it to handle storage, processing, and security requirements.
- **Problems with data quality:** Insights become valuable to the quality of data. Raw data is usually disorganized and unclean and hence hard to analyze. Otherwise, incorrect and irrelevant data may result in unreliable conclusions and ineffective decision-making.
- **Compliance violations:** The responsibility that comes with working with a lot of sensitive data is a big burden. Companies should verify that they adhere to privacy regulations and rules, which might be tricky and difficult to implement in a large data solution.
- **Complexity of integration:** Information is commonly distributed on several platforms and systems. The only challenge is to integrate these different sources into a system that will be effective but it will need to be done to derive the meaningful value.
- **Security issues:** Big data systems contain vital data, and therefore present desirable victims of cyber-attacks. With such complicated environments, good security levels are much needed but not necessarily an achievable objective.

3.1.4 Big Data Strategies and Solutions

Understanding your goals, pinpointing Developing a good data strategy starts with Using the data you currently have and identifying certain use cases. In order to achieve your company's objectives and the systems you'll need to support them; you'll also need to determine what more data and new tools might be needed. Big data technologies can assist with the amount of data gathered, its complexity or diversity, and the pace at which an organization can access the data for analysis.

For example, data lakes receive, analyses, and store any size of original format of semi-structured, unstructured, and structured data. Many Data lakes provide the foundation for several forms of intelligent analytics, including as machine learning, real-time analytics, and visualizations.

Remembering that there isn't a big data strategy that suits everyone is crucial. What is effective for one company may not be the greatest approach another your particular circumstances.

The following four ideas are crucial for developing a successful big data strategy:

- **Open:** Organizations today require the autonomy to create what they want using the resources and solutions they want. Several clouds as information, open-source technology stacks, and interfaces are all part of the reality of big data sources continue to expand and new technological advancements become accessible. To enable businesses to develop the solutions and obtain the data they want to succeed, big data platforms must be designed to be both open and flexible.
- **Intelligent:** In order to employ AI, ML, and smart analytics technologies to save time and effort, big data requires data skills while managing your entire big data infrastructure and providing insights that enhance business decisions. For instance, you should think about automating procedures or allowing self-service analytics so that individuals may handle data independently with little assistance from other teams.
- **Flexible:** Big data analytics should encourage rather than impede innovation. This necessitates creating a data foundation that will integrate data in order to provide on-demand access to storage and computer resources, as well as to make them easy to find and use. Furthermore, it's essential to be able to choose technologies and solutions that fit the workload and use case in order to create the best data toolkits are simple to integrate and utilize in tandem.

- **Trusted:** Big data needs to be trusted in order to be valuable. Building trust in your data—faith that it is accurate, pertinent, and secure—is therefore essential. Data should be secure by default regardless of its source, and your plan should take into account the security features required to guarantee compliance, redundancy, and dependability.

3.2 Apache Hadoop Ecosystem

Large datasets can be distributed stored and processed across computer clusters utilizing the open-source Apache Hadoop program, which makes use of basic concepts in programming. With each server providing local processing in terms of storage capacity, Hadoop is built to grow from a single computer to thousands of clustered devices. Large databases with sizes ranging from gigabytes to petabytes can be effectively stored and processed using Hadoop in this manner.

Hadoop helps in the distribution of huge volumes of data in clusters of commodity hardware, which provides an effective and scalable management of data. Simultaneously, processing of data is done on a group of servers, thus improving performance and minimizing processing time.

The data is first loaded in Hadoop using software clients. "Hadoop Distributed File System" (HDFS) takes care of the distributed storage and metadata. This is followed by processing and transforming the data using MapReduce that performs parallel calculations. Also, YARN (Yet Another Resource Negotiator) handles the resources and allocates them by distributing the computational tasks across the cluster.

One of the core values of all the Hadoop modules is the possibility of the framework to struggle with frequent hardware failures. The system will be configured to automatically identify and tolerate the failure of individual nodes or cluster of machines hence reliability and continuity of data processing.

3.2.1 Hadoop Architecture and Core Components

Hadoop is an open-source platform for processing and preserving enormous amounts of data. Its foundation is Java. Hadoop divides complex analytics and data chores into manageable chunks completed concurrently utilising distributed storage and parallel computation.

The main Hadoop framework is made up of four components that make up the Hadoop ecosystem:

- **Hadoop Distributed File System (HDFS):** The main Hadoop distributed file system is HDFS. It allows every node to use locally stored information thus minimizing the network latency and facilitating high-throughput access to application data. Moreover, HDFS does not require administration define the schema upfront and this gives a more flexibility in processing data of various types.
- **Yet another resource negotiator (YARN):** YARN is a tool of managing resources that is used in managing computing resources in a cluster. It takes care of booking user applications and the allocation of resources to ensure that the Hadoop system is well utilized.
- **MapReduce:** MapReduce is a programming paradigm that is used to handle high amounts of data. Here, big datasets are split into small subsets that are spread among several nodes to be processed concurrently. All the nodes perform their assigned duties simultaneously. Once the processing is done, the intermediate results get consolidated to generate a simplified and manageable set of results.
- **Hadoop Common:** Hadoop Common: Hadoop common is a collection of common libraries and utilities used to facilitate the work of the other modules in the Hadoop ecosystem.

In addition to HDFS, YARN and MapReduce, the Hadoop open-source ecosystem has gone a notch higher to accommodate a wide variety of tools and applications that provide the support of collecting, storing, processing, analyzing and managing massive data. Among which stand out such components as Presto, Apache Zeppelin, Apache Spark, Apache Hive, Apache HBase, and Apache Pig.

3.2.2 The benefits of Hadoop

- **Scalability:** Hadoop is an essential tool for efficiently storing and analyzing massive volumes of data. It does this by using a distributed computing approach that allows for quick data processing that can be quickly increased by adding more computing nodes.

- **Low cost:** Because Hadoop is an inexpensive method of handling and storing data, it is an open-source framework with a vast ecosystem of tools that can operate on commodity hardware massive volumes of data.
- **Flexibility:** Hadoop's versatility in data storage allows a company to retain and utilize as much data as they choose because it doesn't require preprocessing.
- **Resilience:** In the event that one of the hardware nodes fails, Hadoop's distributed computing strategy reroutes workloads to other nodes, enabling fault tolerance and system resilience. Data saved is replicated across multiple system nodes on a single Hadoop cluster to protect against any hardware or software malfunctions.

3.2.3 Challenges of Hadoop

1. **MapReduce complexity and limitations:** MapReduce is a file-intensive system, it could be difficult to use for intricate tasks like interactive analysis. Furthermore, MapReduce features have a steep learning curve and must be developed in Java. Choosing which tools to utilize might be challenging due to the size of the MapReduce ecosystem, which has numerous components for various tasks.
2. **Security:** Because Hadoop manages such massive numbers, Data security and sensitivity could be issues. To help developers safeguard data in Hadoop, an ecosystem of tools for encryption, auditing, provisioning, and authentication has emerged.
3. **Governance and management:** Hadoop lacks many reliable solutions for data governance and administration, as well as for data quality and standardization.
4. **Talent gap:** Hadoop is recognized to have a skill gap, just like many other programming specialties. Locating developers who possess the Java knowledge needed to create operating systems, hardware, and MapReduce may be difficult. Additionally, because of its high learning curve, new programmers may find it difficult to grasp MapReduce's environment and recommended practices.

3.2.4 Hadoop tools

The capabilities of the core a wide range the Hadoop module can be enhanced and improved with a variety of open-source technologies. Among the primary software applications utilized with Hadoop are:

- Apache Impala: An open-source SQL enquiry machine that works nicely with Hadoop and processes data in large parallel
- Apache Sqoop: An effective command-line tool for moving enormous amounts of data between relational databases and Hadoop
- Apache Zookeeper: An open-source server that supports reliable distributed coordination in Hadoop by maintaining configuration information, naming, providing distributed synchronization, and providing group services.
- Apache Oozie: A workflow scheduler for Hadoop works.
- Apache Hive: A data warehouse that enables programmers to utilize the SQL-like query language HiveQL to interact with HDFS data.
- Apache HBase: Hadoop is frequently used with this distributed, open-source, non-relational database.
- Apache Pig: This tool facilitates actions like filter, sort, load, and join and is used as an abstraction layer atop MapReduce for processing huge data sets.

3.2.5 Use Cases of Apache Hadoop

A rare common use for Apache Hadoop is as follows:

- **Analytics and big data:** Many companies and organizations utilize Hadoop for research, production data processing, and analytics that require data parallel processing, processing terabytes or petabytes of enormous data, and storing various datasets.
- **Data storage and archiving:** Because Frame storing on product hardware is made possible by Hadoop, which is helpful as a cost-effective storage option for a range of data types, including click torrents, contacts, and device and mechanism facts.
- **Data lakes:** Data lakes, which store enormous amounts of unprocessed data, can be used with Hadoop, since it can assist in storing data without preprocessing.
- **Analytics for marketing:** Customer relationship management

(CRM) data is frequently stored and analyzed by marketing teams using Hadoop.

- **Risk management:** Hadoop is used by to develop risk management and analysis models for financial services firms such as banks and insurance providers.
- **AI and appliance knowledge:** Model training and data processing for appliance knowledge applications are made easier by Hadoop ecosystems.

3.3 Apache Spark for Large-Scale Data Processing

An open-source, high-performance data processing engine called Apache Spark is widely used in large-scale data analytics and machine learning workloads.

Apache Spark, a fast and adaptable gathering machine that works with Spark, makes handling large-scale data sets simple. Specifically for streaming data, graph data, analytics, machine learning, large-scale data processing, and artificial intelligence applications, it is made to offer the computing speed, scalability, and programmability needed for big data.

Spark's in-memory calculation methodology allows it to attain far faster performance than disk-based processing frameworks like Hadoop MapReduce. It features built-in fault tolerance and parallelism, and it grows by spreading out processing tasks across enormous computer clusters. Data scientists and analysts even use its APIs for well-known programming languages like Scala, Java, Python, and R.

Spark and Apache Hadoop are frequently contrasted, particularly in relation to MapReduce, Hadoop's integrated data processing feature. Instead of writing to or reading from disc, Spark processes data and stores it in memory for further stages, resulting in significantly quicker processing speeds. This is the primary difference between Spark and MapReduce.

Currently supported by a substantial and active open-source developer community, it has over 1,000 contributors and is managed by the Foundation for Apache Software. Furthermore, it is an essential component of a number of commercial big data products.

3.3.1 How Apache Spark works

Apache Spark has a very hierarchical design with the control and coordination cascading down to several working nodes under a single authority. The Spark Driver or the master node as it is sometimes known, is at the center of it. It takes the form of the brain to the system- it communicates with the cluster manager; it directs actions and finally provides processed results to the application client.

Upon the application being initiated, Spark Driver will form the Spark Context that forms the entry point to the entire Spark ecosystem. In this context, it is related to cluster managers like Hadoop YARN, Kubernetes, Mesos, or its own standalone manager Spark. These managers aid in the allocation of duties among different nodes and monitoring of their performance.

One of the factors that have contributed to the amazing velocity and output of Spark is the employment of Resilient Distributed Datasets (RDDs). These are distributed data structures which permit the processing of data in parallel on multiple nodes and fault tolerance. Collectively, these elements facilitate Spark to execute big data processing at a rapid pace, reliably, and very well coordinated.

- **Resilient Distributed Dataset (RDD)**

Resilient distributed datasets, It is able to read data directly into the external sources, re-format existing collections into distributed datasets, or it can parallelize data using the Spark Context method to convert the data into RDDs that can be processed. The only difference that is really distinct about Spark is that these RDDs can be processed in memory. Spark stores data in a format that is easily accessible in-memory, thus substantially increasing the speed, which would take repeated disk reads before data is read, instead of only updating the disk when required, or when explicitly told to do so.

RDDs are intelligently divided into logical chunks each of which can be processed by many nodes simultaneously. This is the parallelism of performance of Spark. Furthermore, the users may work with RDDs by two major types of operations: transformations, which generate new datasets out of the current ones, and actions, which generate final results.

Essentially, RDDs simplify the process of large-scale data processing to a smooth, quick and stable process.

Operations that produce a new RDD are called transformations. Apache Spark is instructed to perform computations and utilize actions to provide the driver with the outcome.

Many actions and transformations on RDDs are supported by Spark. Users don't need to bother about choosing the appropriate distribution because Spark handles this.

- **Directed Acyclic Graph (DAG)**

Unlike MapReduce, which executes jobs in two stages, Spark organizes jobs and worker nodes throughout the cluster using a Directed Acyclic Graph (DAG). While Spark acts and updates data during the job execution stages, the DAG scheduler enhances performance by coordinating the worker nodes throughout the cluster. Using the recorded actions in conjunction with the information from an earlier state, this task-tracking enables fault tolerance.

- **Data Frames and Datasets**

Data Frames have become the most mainstream and most commonly used API to work with structured data in the world of Apache Spark. Just like a database table, they present data in rows and columns and it is easy to manipulate. Even though RDDs still play a fundamental role in Spark, they are currently mostly in a maintenance phase with Data Frames becoming the dominant player in the current data processing application.

The integration of Data Frames and the Machine Learning Library (MLlib) of Spark is one of the factors that contributed to this change. The library is also equipped with an extensive collection of scalable machine learning algorithms, tools used to construct efficient ML pipelines, and feature selection. Data Frames have a similar interface on various programming languages: Scala, Java, Python, and R, therefore, they are very versatile and can be used by developers with different backgrounds.

In contrast to Data Frames, which are untyped, Dataset is a strongly typed object of the Java Virtual machine and is more type-safe and less prone to error in the development process.

Spark SQL can be used to query data from SQL data stores like Apache Hive and Data Frames. A Data Frame or Dataset is produced when Spark SQL queries are run in a different language.

- **Spark Core**

The Apache Spark relies on Spark Core to execute all the parallel data processing. It deals with scheduling of tasks, optimization, RDDs and data abstraction. It also provides the support of important libraries of Spark like Spark SQL, Spark streaming, MLlib and graphX, on which they operate. Spark Core offers faster, easier, and efficient processing of big data by abstracting and managing information that is spread out in clusters.

- **Spark APIs**

To enable as many individuals as possible to utilize Spark's power, there are several application programming interfaces (APIs) available for Spark. Relational interaction with RDD data is made possible by Spark SQL. Additionally, Spark's Python, R, Java, and Scala APIs are thoroughly documented. There are minor variations in data management for each language API in Spark. Every language API offers RDDs, Data Frames, and Datasets.

3.3.2 Advantages of Apache Spark

Spark accelerates operations and development in a number of ways. Teams will benefit from Spark:

- **Quicken app expansion:** Building apps that take advantage of machine learning and graph analytics is made simpler by MLlib and GraphX support the Streaming and SQL programming paradigms of Apache Spark.
- **Innovate more quickly:** APIs make it simple to manipulate and alter semi-structured data.
- **Easily manage:** SQL queries, graph processing, streaming data, and machine learning (ML) are all supported by a single engine.
- **Optimize using open technologies:** To maximize performance for Apache Spark workloads, the Open POWER Foundation makes RDMA, FPGA acceleration, GPU, CAPI Flash, and machine learning innovation are all feasible.

- **Process quicker:** Because Spark uses an in-memory processing paradigm, it can operate noticeably faster than disk-based frameworks like Hadoop MapReduce.

3.3.3 Apache Spark and Machine Learning

Stream processing, artificial intelligence, and machine learning are among the many libraries that enhance Spark's capabilities.

- **Apache Spark MLlib:** Among the most significant aspects Spark MLlib, an integrated solution for performing classification and regression, collaborative filtering, clustering, distributed linear algebra, decision trees, random forests, gradient-boosted trees, frequent pattern mining, evaluation metrics, and statistics, is one of Apache Spark's machine learning features. Apache Spark is an essential big data tool due to the MLlib's capabilities and the variety of data sources it supports.
- **Spark GraphX:** In addition to being able to use APIs, Graph problems are the focus of Spark GraphX. GraphX is a graph abstraction that extends RDDs for graphs and graph-parallel processing. Graph databases that store webs of connections or interconnectivity data, such as those found in social networks, can be integrated with Spark GraphX.
- **Spark Streaming:** Scalable, Fault-tolerant processing of real-time data streams is made possible via Spark Streaming, an extension of the core Spark API. Spark Streaming uses Spark's machine learning and graph-processing algorithms to analyses data and disseminate it to file systems, databases, and real-time streaming analytics dashboards. Additionally, Spark Streaming, which is built on the Spark SQL engine, makes incremental batch processing possible and accelerates the processing of streamed data.

3.4 Data Storage Technologies for Big Data

Big data storage involves collecting, managing, and storing enormous, complex datasets that traditional systems can't handle due to their volume, velocity, and variety. Solutions use scalable architectures, such are distributed file systems and cloud-based object storage, such Azure Blob Storage or

Amazon S3, to handle enormous volumes of organized and unstructured data. Key considerations include scalability, cost, performance, durability, security, and compliance with regulations.

Core components of big data systems:

1. **Scalable architecture:** Big data stowage requires a flexible, scalable infrastructure that can grow with the data.
2. **Distributed storage**: Large datasets are often distributed across many servers and high-capacity disks to manage the volume effectively.
3. **Object storage**: On-premise object storage platforms compatible with the S3 interface.
4. **Data lakes:** Centralized storage solutions that store data in its original form, enabling various analytics, including machine learning.
5. **Data warehouses:** Systems that aggregate data from different sources for robust analysis and data mining.
6. **NoSQL databases:** Databases like Cassandra or MongoDB that are made to manage massive amounts of diverse data, providing low-latency access.

3.4.1 Core Components of Big Data Storage

1. Data Lakes

A data lake serves as a central storage system which retains unprocessed data until its required time of use. Data lakes enable organizations to process incoming data because they accept data from all sources without requiring any specific format, this comprises organized, unstructured, and semi-structured data. The system makes it possible for to gather extensive data by collecting information from various sources such as logs and images and videos and IoT device outputs.

The primary benefit of data lakes arises from their ability to operate at low costs since they utilize standard storage solutions and cloud-based object storage systems. The process of data lake management demands organizations to implement strict data governance procedures, which help prevent data swamp conditions that result from disorganized data storage and missing metadata.

2. Data Warehouses

Data warehouses function as dedicated storage systems which handle analytical tasks and reporting requirements for extensive collections of structured data. The system implements schema-on-write which requires data to undergo cleaning and transformation processes before it can be stored. The system provides rapid and uniform query execution capabilities which make data warehouses ideal for business intelligence operations and reporting functions.

Data warehouses typically employ relational database systems that have been optimized or columnar storage systems to enable users to perform complex SQL operations and data aggregation tasks. Organizations use data warehouses to conduct high-speed analytics because their queries involve performing joins and grouping operations on extensive datasets. Data warehouses excel at processing structured data but they cannot match the flexible capabilities offered by data lakes.

3. Object Storage

Every object in object storage contains its actual data together with its associated metadata and a distinct identifier which results in a flat data storage system. Object storage functions as a system that stores unstructured data which includes audio and video files and document and image content.

Big data workloads which need data processing framework integration and high durability and resilience will find object storage as their ideal solution. The system provides automatic management capabilities which include versioning and access control and lifecycle management which enables users to manage petabyte-sized data collections with ease. Object storage does not provide optimal performance for handling transactional workloads because it lacks the capability to deliver rapid processing speeds and multiple input/output operations per second.

4. Distributed File Systems

By spreading data across multiple physical nodes, distributed file systems (DFS) provide redundancy, scalability, and parallel access to large datasets. Applications are shielded from the intricacies of network failures and hardware layout by DFS. To maintain data availability and consistency, these systems employ strategies including fault detection, data replication, and sharding. Many large-scale analytics pipelines rely on DFS, which allows processing frameworks to receive and write data simultaneously from several nodes. Although DFS provides scalability and resilience, load balancing and consistency maintenance become more difficult.

5. Relational and NoSQL Databases

Relational databases which use structured schemas and SQL continue to serve essential functions for big data applications because of their ability to maintain strong data consistency and their support for transactional processes and established software systems. Data which has diverse characteristics or rapid changes in its properties cannot be managed by these systems because they fail to achieve horizontal scalability. The development of NoSQL databases, such as columnar, graph, document, and key-value databases has developed as a solution to these issues.

NoSQL databases enable the storage of unstructured and semi-structured data while delivering scalable performance for cloud-native distributed workloads. The system handles both read-heavy and write-heavy operations and flexible-schema scenarios to enable big data applications which range from real-time messaging through to extensive content management. The decision to use relational or NoSQL database systems depends on three factors which include transaction requirements and consistency models and the type of data being stored.

3.4.2 Big Data Storage Technologies

1. Hadoop and HDFS

The HDFS a scalable folder organization intended for massive batch processing, is the foundation of the Hadoop ecosystem. To guarantee high availability and fault tolerance, HDFS replicates files across several nodes by dividing them into big blocks. Many data processing frameworks, including MapReduce, Hive, and Spark, are built on this paradigm, which facilitates parallel execution by dividing computation and storage.

HDFS allows storage of both structured and unstructured data, efficiently managing petabytes of information across commodity hardware.

Its focus on throughput over single-record latency makes it suitable for data mining, ETL, and batch analytics. However, it is less suited for workloads requiring low-latency random access or extensive metadata operations.

2. Object Store

Big data operations depend on cloud object storage services because they provide Scalable and long-lasting storage options that integrate easily with analytics and machine learning services are offered by Amazon S3, Google Cloud Storage, and Azure Blob Storage. The facilities enable organizations to grow their operations because they eliminate the need for organizations to spend money on fundamental hardware components. On-prem object stores which provides reduced costs, full data sovereignty, and enhanced performance vs cloud.

Data is stored as discrete objects which contain their separate metadata and can be accessed through RESTful APIs for programmatic use. Object stores provide built-in capabilities such as access control, replication across geographic regions, and automated lifecycle management.

3. Columnar / Analytical Storage

The columnar storage systems store data in columns which deliver better reading and aggregation speed for analytical tasks that require specific column access. Popular examples include Amazon Redshift, Google BigQuery, Apache Parquet, and Apache ORC. The systems achieve better compression through their contiguous column storage which also decreases I/O demands to speed up complex analytical queries across extensive datasets. Columnar stores are ideal for activities involving OLAP (online analytical processing), where users carry out operations like filtering, grouping, and aggregation over billions of entries. The system performs better for analytics purposes although it does not handle transactional (OLTP) workloads efficiently.

4. Cold Storage

Cold storage is designed for infrequently accessed, archival data, such as compliance records, historical backups, or raw sensor logs that must be retained for regulatory or legal reasons but do not require active processing. Tape drives and optical discs and specialized cloud storage tiers like

Amazon Glacier or Azure Archive Storage function as standard cold storage solutions which deliver much lower storage costs per terabyte than active storage tiers.

The main advantage of cold storage comes with its primary disadvantage because users experience extended wait times when they try to access data. Cold storage systems provide users with automated lifecycle management systems which move data from hot or warm storage tiers to cold storage when its access rate decreases. The three factors of retrieval speed and retention requirements and costs need to be balanced by organizations when they create their cold storage systems for big data.

5. SSD, NVMe, Persistent Memory, NVRAM

The storage of big data received a revolutionizing update through Solid-State Drives with their NVMe technologies and persistent memory and NVRAM storage. The use of SSDs originated as a method to enhance performance for high-end servers but nowadays storage arrays and distributed databases and caching layers all utilize SSD technology. The use of NVMe drives enables users to retrieve data faster because they connect directly to the server's PCIe bus which eliminates the need for standard storage controllers. Persistent memory and NVRAM technologies create a new form of storage because they allow data to stay intact after power outages while creating access speeds similar to RAM. The Tier-0 storage system which combines caching with transaction logs and metadata requires these technologies for its fast performance needs. The price of storage space for these products exceeds the cost of traditional HDD storage and cloud storage services.

6. Caching, Tiering, and Hierarchical Storage Management (HSM)

Caching uses fast memory or SSD technology to keep commonly used data, which helps to decrease reading times in large data operations. Storage software or hardware appliances handle automatic data movement between different storage classes according to user access patterns. The system places hot data on SSD or NVMe storage while it transfers cold data to less expensive, slower storage. Hierarchical storage management (HSM) systems use this concept to automatically shift data between different storage locations and archival storage areas based on data access frequency and business requirements and data age. HSM enables organizations to manage their big data operations because it supports data management from immediate access to permanent storage.

3.4.3 Use Cases of Big Data Storage

1. Financial Services

Financial services enterprises utilize big data storage to manage and analyze extensive trading data together with transaction logs and customer activity data in real-time. The three systems which need fast-access storage solutions include high-frequency trading algorithms and fraud detection systems and regulatory compliance workloads. The systems need to achieve high reliability together with data protection while they store multiple petabytes of data for audit purposes and risk assessment activities.

Banks and investment firms use data lakes and warehouses to support their credit scoring and portfolio management and personalized marketing analytics. Financial data storage needs special security measures which include access restrictions and adherence to regulations like GDPR and PCI DSS.

2. Healthcare and Life Sciences

Healthcare and life sciences Organisations use Wearable technology, genomic sequencing, medical imaging, and electronic health records (EHR) to produce enormous volumes of data. Solutions for storing big data must not only handle the volume and diversity of this information but also ensure privacy compliance with regulations like HIPAA. Object and distributed file storage underpin clinical research, telemedicine analytics, and patient data management.

Life sciences research, such as drug discovery or genomics, demands high-throughput storage systems capable of supporting specialized workloads, often involving large files and multidimensional data. Robust metadata management and data governance are crucial for ensuring data lineage, reproducibility, and collaboration across research teams.

3. IoT and Sensor Data

The increasing number of IoT devices which include industrial sensors smart meters connected vehicles and consumer wearables creates an ongoing requirement for specialized options for data storage that can manage their constant flow of data. IoT devices need storage options that can write data quickly and multiple data structures while providing real-time analytics for detecting anomalies and monitoring trends.

The adoption of distributed storage systems combined with cloud-native architectures has become standard practice because these systems make it easier to transfer data between devices and cloud infrastructure while maintaining data storage capabilities. The long-term preservation of sensor data becomes necessary for developing predictive maintenance systems which fulfill regulatory standards and enable historical trend assessments. Organizations use cold storage together with intelligent data lifecycle management to reduce expenses because many IoT datasets become unusable after a certain period.

4. Media and Entertainment

Petabytes of high-resolution video, music, photos, and user-engagement data are handled by media and entertainment companies. Workflows for content generation, archives, and content delivery networks (CDNs) that need low-latency access to big media assets are made possible by big data storage. While distributed file systems facilitate collaborative editing and production workflows, object storage is frequently utilized for original video and completed assets.

Personalisation, audience segmentation, and targeted advertising are made possible by analytics on massive user data. For quick access to both content and metadata, this combines data lakes, analytical warehouses, and caching.

5. Government and Public Sector

Big data storage is used by government organizations to maintain open data portals, criminal databases, census information, and geographical data. In addition to scaling to handle massive information, storage solutions must adhere to strict legal, privacy, and categorization standards. Agencies may publish, retrieve, and safeguard vast volumes of sensitive and public data with the aid of distributed storage and cloud-based object storage.

Disaster response analytics, fraud detection, urban planning, and citizen engagement platforms are examples of public sector workloads that are powered by data-intensive procedures. In order to keep long-term records for accountability and transparency and to guarantee high availability during emergencies, effective storage management is necessary.

3.4.4 Important Considerations When Choosing a Big Data Storage Solution

Organizations should consider the following factors when selecting a storage solution for big data use cases.

- **Scalability**

Any big data storage solution requires scalability as its most important feature. Organizations must anticipate rapid growth in data volume and user demand, choosing systems that scale horizontally across nodes instead of vertically through individual machine upgrades. Distributed file systems and object storage systems provide organizations with a solution to expand their infrastructure through server or cloud resource additions, which enables them to avoid expensive hardware replacement procedures.

When organizations encounter changes in their workload requirements and their data retention policies, they need to use scalable architectures for their business needs. Organizations use cloud storage because it enables dedicated storage space that expands during temporary usage spikes and permanent growth, while on-premises systems need organizations to assess their storage needs through meticulous capacity assessments. The core requirement for assessing big data storage solutions demands that systems should have the ability to grow capacity without causing any service interruptions or system slowdowns.

- **Data Volume, Velocity, and Variety**

Big data storage solutions must be engineered for the “three Vs”: volume (size), velocity (rate of ingress), and variety (diverse formats). Modern workloads may generate terabytes or petabytes per day, requiring both high-throughput ingestion and long-term archiving. Rapid ingestion capabilities are crucial for use cases like real-time analytics, while volume influences storage architecture and cost.

Variety refers to the range of data types, from structured tables to images, video, and machine logs. Storage platforms must flexibly handle this diversity, often support schema-less or semi-organized data, as well as provide metadata management to enable search, analysis, and governance.

- **Performance**

Performance in big data storage involves the capacity to swiftly read and write vast amounts of data, even when several users or programs are accessing it at once. Real-time requires high throughput and minimal latency analytics, streaming ingestion, and fast query execution. This is achieved through parallel I/O operations, optimized data formats (like columnar storage), and integration with compute engines that process data in place.

Storage systems must also support consistent performance as data scales. Factors such as network bandwidth, IOPS, block size, and indexing strategies all play a role. For analytics-heavy workloads, performance tuning might involve balancing read and write patterns, leveraging in-memory caching, and reducing unnecessary data movement through co-located compute and storage.

- **Cost**

Cost control is a persistent concern, as big data storage needs can scale unpredictably. Direct costs include hardware, software licenses, and cloud storage fees, while indirect expenses cover energy, maintenance, and administrative overhead. It's important to account for not only up-front capital expenses (CapEx) but ongoing operating costs (OpEx) tied to egress, data retrieval, and backup.

Tiered storage, cloud pay-per-use models, and automated lifecycle management help optimize expenditure by aligning cost with actual access patterns and retention needs. Pricing transparency and flexibility, such as the ability to move data between storage classes, are essential to avoid vendor lock-in and support evolving data strategies.

- **Durability and Availability**

Durability refers to the long-term persistence and integrity of data, even in the face of hardware failures or system crashes. Big data storage systems achieve durability through replication, erasure coding, and distributed architectures that reduce the possibility of data loss. Cloud providers typically offer durability SLAs measured in "nines" (e.g., 99.999999999%) to ensure critical data is preserved across failures and disasters.

Availability measures how reliably users and systems can access data when needed. Redundant storage nodes, multi-zone or multi-region replication, and failover mechanisms are essential to maintain uptime, especially for mission-critical applications. Systems must also support online scaling and maintenance without disrupting access, ensuring high availability during upgrades or infrastructure changes.

- **Security and Compliance**

Security is non-negotiable in big data storage. Organizations deal with sensitive and regulated information, so storage platforms must provide robust mechanisms for access control, encryption at rest and in transit, audit logging, and intrusion detection. The distributed nature of big data increases the attack surface and potential vulnerabilities, so layered security is critical.

Compliance adds further complexity, especially for industries governed by laws such as GDPR, HIPAA, or sector-specific mandates on data retention, locality, and sharing. Storage solutions should support granular data governance, legal hold, and automated enforcement of data lifecycle and privacy rules.

- **Data Model Compatibility**

Data model compatibility ensures storage technologies can efficiently manage the organization's data types and workload patterns. For example, objects, documents, time series, graphs, and tabular data each have different requirements for access, indexing, and querying. A poor match can lead to costly workaround solutions or reduced performance. Relational databases offer rigor for structured data, while NoSQL and object stores handle unstructured and evolving formats.

Integration with analytics engines, ETL tools, and data science frameworks is also impacted by how well the storage system aligns with the models in use. The flexibility to evolve data models over time becomes important as business needs and data sources change. Evaluating compatibility at both the storage and application layers is key to a future-proof big data architecture.

3.5 Real-Time Data Streaming Technologies

Real-time data streaming refers to the instant processing of data points as they arrive—often milliseconds after they're generated.

This low-latency approach is distinct from traditional batch processing, in which tasks are grouped together and executed during scheduled times. In contrast, through streaming data in real time, the instantaneous processing of "data in motion" means enterprises can access fresh, up-to-the-minute information. Real-time sources of data include:

- Internet of Things (IoT) devices and sensors
- Financial market data feeds
- Social media
- Point-of-sale and e-commerce systems
- Clickstreams (records of user behavior on a website)

Analysis of such information produces insights that can power timely decision-making and real-time applications, including agentic artificial intelligence. Additional benefits of real-time data streaming include improved operational efficiency, data retention, risk management and customer personalization.

Real-time data streaming is made possible by an infrastructure consisting of an ingestion layer, a real-time processing engine and a storage and serving layer. Solutions such as open-source frameworks and data streaming platforms support real-time streaming infrastructure and help enterprises efficiently manage millions of records across thousands of data pipelines.

3.5.1 Importance of Real-Time Data Streaming

Organizations often struggle to process high-velocity data streams using traditional batch processing methods.

Such is the dilemma enterprises face when trying to harness the power of fast-moving streams of information—one of the most valuable sources of business intelligence today.

Real-time data streaming offers enterprises a way to leverage real-time data fast, without the mess.

Businesses utilize real-time data ingestion and processing to stream continuous data into their real-time analytics systems which generate immediate actionable insights. The ability to access real-time insights gives businesses from various industries and fields a competitive edge. Retailers use real-time customer demand data to make immediate changes to their pricing systems. Banks use their transaction data to conduct real-time fraud detection operations. Manufacturers use their systems to find machine breakdowns which they resolve before their machines face extended operational halts.

The capability of businesses to use their data in real-time becomes more powerful when they combine it with agentic AI technology. Agentic AI uses real-time information to enable machines to make independent decisions in the actual world which include discovering and countering cybersecurity threats and changing shipping paths when traffic jams occur. Organizations cannot obtain these advantages without using real-time data streaming technology. They would depend on outdated methods to collect and analyze data which operate at reduced speeds.

3.5.2 Benefits of Real-Time Data Streaming

Enterprises that use real-time data streaming experience many benefits, including:

- **Better decision-making:**

Fresh information can yield more accurate insights, especially in situations where even hours-old data could be considered stale, whether it comes to healthcare or stock trading. With incoming real-time data, businesses are also empowered to make decisions for operational efficiency, such as identifying and addressing production bottlenecks.

- **Smarter data retention**

Too often, companies ingest and retain large volumes of data that they don't actually need. Such "data hoarding" can mean the accumulation of duplicate records that consume costly storage space, undermine data analysis projects and become an overall drag on system performance.

But early filtering enabled by real-time data streaming can help organizations avoid storing redundant data, reducing the likelihood of data hoarding and its consequences.

- **Predictive analytics**

Enterprises can integrate historical data with real-time streaming data to support predictive analytics. This holistic form of data analysis can support use cases such as smart farming practices and personalized customer experiences.

Predictive analytics powered by real-time data can also improve risk management: Access to time-sensitive data on dangerous weather conditions to suspicious financial transactions can help enterprises spot and mitigate threats to their operations and bottom lines.

3.5.3 What is streaming architecture?

The data architecture that supports real-time data streaming is streaming architecture, with data engineering components designed to keep data moving and avoid staleness. The three basic components are: 1) Ingestion, 2) Processing, and 3) Destination

1. Ingestion

Various sources continuously produce and emit data points. This incoming data is often unbounded, meaning it is generated and continues flowing without a fixed endpoint. That information is captured by data ingestion tools with streaming connectors and then delivered to a processor. "Application programming interfaces" (APIs) can also help automate the transmission of real-time data from various sources.

2. Processing

Real-time data processing is another name for stream processing, involves filtering, enriching, transforming, or analyzing data as it comes in. Data analysis can be powered by AI and machine learning and discern patterns and other key insights.

3. Destination

The processed data is delivered to a destination for either immediate use (in an app or dashboard, for instance) or storage. Organizations often rely on data lakes and data lake houses for the storage of streaming data because they can accommodate high volumes of data at relatively low costs. Streaming data can also be stored in ETL (extract, transform, load) procedures are used in data warehouses for data transformation, organization and visualization.

3.5.4 Real-time data streaming considerations

To successfully leverage present data streaming, it can be helpful to consider and plan for challenges inherent in its implementation.

- **Costs and resource utilization:** On-demand data ingestion, processing and analytics—especially for massive, complex volumes of data, also known as big data—are expensive and resource-intensive endeavors. In determining whether to commit funding and resources to real-time data streaming, enterprises should balance its costs against the costs of stale data and slower decision-making.
- **Ensuring fault tolerance:** Successful real-time data streaming depends on a system's fault tolerance, or its capacity to keep running even when a component fails. Real-time data interruptions and outages streaming systems could result in data loss while undermining the speed that distinguishes streaming from other processing methods.
- **Maintaining observability:** Comprehensive views into streaming data pipelines are necessary to avoid pipeline failures and ensure optimal performance. Monitoring key data quality metrics and quickly identifying problems—such as schema changes and data drift—can help enterprises ensure data integrity and pipeline reliability.
- **Security and governance:** Sensitive data can be continuously flowing through real-time data streaming or Data privacy laws apply to "personally identifiable information" (PII). Measures to ensure secure pipelines, including data encryption and access controls, can help enterprises adhere to regulatory regimes and avoid data breaches.

Multiple Choice Questions (MCQs)

1. **Which of the following is a key characteristic of Big Data?**
   A. Small volume of structured data
   B. High cost of storage only
   C. Volume, Velocity, Variety
   D. Manual data processing

2. **Which programming model is primarily used in Apache Hadoop for distributed data processing?**
   A. SQL
   B. MapReduce
   C. JavaFX
   D. REST API

3. **In the Hadoop ecosystem, which component is responsible for distributed storage?**
   A. Hive
   B. Pig
   C. HDFS
   D. Sqoop

4. **Which Hadoop ecosystem tool is mainly used for querying large datasets using an SQL-like language?**
   A. Flume
   B. Hive
   C. Oozie
   D. Zookeeper

5. **What is one major advantage of Apache Spark over Hadoop MapReduce?**
   A. It only works with structured data
   B. It processes data only in batch mode
   C. It supports in-memory computation
   D. It does not support machine learning

6. **Which of the following is a core component of Apache Spark?**
   A. Spark SQL
   B. HDFS NameNode
   C. HBase Master
   D. YARN ResourceManager

7. **Which NoSQL database is commonly used in Big Data environments for column-oriented storage?**
   A. MySQL
   B. Oracle
   C. HBase
   D. PostgreSQL

8. **Which data storage technology is best suited for storing semi-structured and unstructured Big Data?**
   A. Traditional relational databases only
   B. NoSQL databases
   C. Spreadsheet software
   D. Desktop file systems

9. **Which of the following technologies is widely used for real-time data streaming in Big Data systems?**
   A. Apache Kafka
   B. Apache Pig
   C. Apache Mahout
   D. Apache Avro

10. What is the main purpose of real-time data streaming technologies?

A. To store only historical data

B. To process data as it is generated

C. To replace all databases

D. To reduce internet speed

Answers

1	2	3	4	5	6	7	8	9	10
C	B	C	B	C	A	C	B	A	B

CHAPTER 4

DATA ENGINEERING AND DATA PIPELINES

4.1 MODERN DATA ENGINEERING PRACTICES

Contemporary data engineering has progressed in parallel with the development in the software development methodology. The use of data-driven decision-making in organizations has led to increased focus on efficient, scalable, and reliable data systems to support the organization. Conventional methods of data management fail to manage the increasing complexity of data, capacity of data, and speed of data. To overcome these issues, data engineering is becoming more DevOps-inspired, including using automation, collaboration, constant integration, and delivering data products quickly (AL-Jumaili et al., 2023). The goals of these practices are to progress the data quality, provide reproducibility, and reduce the development patterns, which will narrow the divide between data engineering and modern software engineering processes.

KEY TAKEAWAYS

- **Requirements for data engineering DevOps-like practices:** Through continuous feedback loops, CI/CD, and collaboration, DevOps made it possible for data teams to create, deliver, and maintain data products at the same pace as software.
- **Collaboration and recovery are made possible by data versioning:** Teams may work independently, replicate failures, and swiftly recover from mistakes without affecting production data thanks to versioned data includes time travel, branching, and merging.
- **Data can benefit from the application of CI/CD concepts:** hooks, pre-merge checks, and automation tests can ensure that defective

data does not make it to production, allowing for the ongoing delivery of first-rate data goods.

- **Reproducible root-cause study and regaining is necessary for resilience:** that is, data state reproducibility is necessary for testing and development, particularly while resolving data quality problems.
- **Tooling:** Putting best practices into practice: Only with specialised data version management solutions can concepts like data versioning and CI/CD be used to accommodate a vast amount of data and a variety of workflows.

The shift in package manufacturing which has taken place in the past periods, particularly in the framework of the rejection of the conventional models employed in the waterfall to the DevOps one has impacted the modern data engineering. Devops promotes continuous development, integration and deployment such that the software is deployable at any one moment. Version control systems, continuous integration systems, and containerization technologies are also such tools that have assisted in this transition and helped in collaboration, automation, and efficient delivery. The same principles are being embraced in data engineering in order to enhance reliability and scalability of data systems.

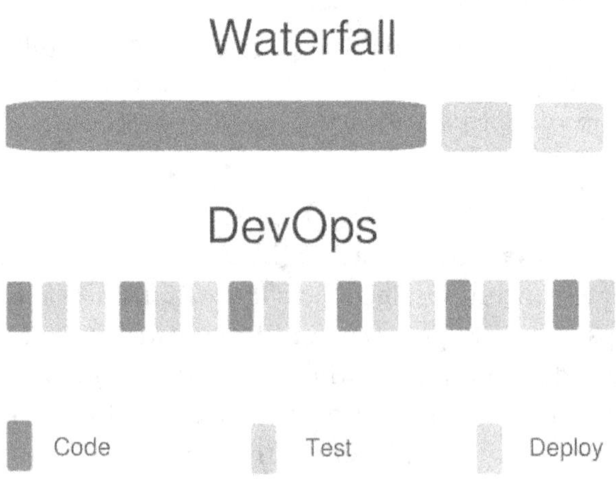

Figure 4.1: Development Processes

Source: (Orr, 2026)

4.1.1 Evolution of Data Engineering

In order for data scientists to extract useful insights from vast amounts of raw, structured, semi-structured, and unstructured data, the area of data engineering develops methods for collecting, storing, processing, and analyzing such data.

Data engineering includes both access assurance and data quality. Before loading data and beginning data processing processes, data engineers must ensure that data sets from various data sources, such as data warehouses, are complete and clean.

Additionally, they have to guarantee that data consumers (such business analysts and data scientists) may easily access and query the prepared data using technologies that are chosen by data scientists and data analytics.

Over time, the field of data engineering has also experienced numerous revolutions, and new tools and technologies have been developed to meet the expanding demands of this field.

This domain has changed in a number of ways, including:

- The shift increasing variety of data types that required to be saved led to a shift from tabular, structured data to unstructured data and data storage. The requirement to use computation and analytics engines to develop complex algorithms and analytics has been fueled by the increasing need for AI in all digital applications.
- The creation of cutting-edge the variety of sources and technology that enable ETLs and streaming from every imaginable data source the requirement for infinitely fast distributed data input.
- The necessity to create and manage sophisticated AI algorithms for large-scale production systems gave rise to the emergence of AI and ML tools that make it possible to operationalize algorithm creation as much as possible. These are only a few of the developments in this discipline.

4.1.2 Data Engineering Tools

Software programs and platforms that support the creation, administration, and optimization of data pipelines are known as data engineering tools. Data intake, processing, transformation, storage, orchestration, and monitoring are just a few of the phases of the data lifecycle that these technologies cover. They ensure the smooth flow of information in a business, starting with raw data towards processed data to report, analyze or machine learn.

Various solutions to data engineering problems include dealing with big data environments. As an illustration, orchestration tools automate the process, ingestion tools collect the data and processing tools clean and transform it. By integrating storage, governance, and monitoring systems, organizations can develop effective, safe and scalable data pipelines, which could be used to support a wide range of business requirements.

Types of Data Engineering Tools

1. Ingestion Tools

The ingestion tools have the responsibility of bringing together data in a single system out of a myriad of glues such as databases, streaming services, and APIs. They allow the entry of data to be processed into processing systems, data lakes or data warehouses through the management of both batch and real-time data inflow.

Such technologies will be able to ensure the effective gathering of raw data based on multiple sources and its further processing and analysis. They are also dealing with the challenges of various types data and reliable and scalable data ingestion.

2. Processing Tools

Processing tools are used to manipulate raw data to be prepared to be analyzed or stored. These tools perform these tasks of filtering, sorting and aggregation of data typically across distributed systems. They are able to process large volumes of data in batch and real-time systems, requiring businesses to handle massive amounts of data an effective manner.

Processing tools aid in transforming raw or semi-structured data into more polished data, which is easier to extract insights out of, deploy machine learning models, or produce comprehensive reports.

3. Transformation Tools

The transformation tools organize and standardize the raw data. In order to guarantee the data is readable and accurate, this can include data cleaning, normalizing, and de-duplicating information and other data quality enhancements.

Transformation tools are used to make sure that data can be used to satisfy the downstream demands of a data format like analytics or reporting systems. Transforming data can be standardized and automated to ensure data is accurate and reliable across all systems.

4. Orchestration Tools

Data workflow execution and coordination is to be done using a tool of instrumentation to ensure that the different tasks, such as ingesting data, processing data, and transforming data, take place in the proper order. They assist in scheduling, tracking and optimization of complex data pipelines, task dependencies.

Orchestration tools are aimed to ensure the effective and easy functioning of the workflows, even though the number of data pipelines is going to be increased. They also provide resilience to failures of their data pipelines through error handling and recovery.

5. Storage and Integration Tools.

Large volumes of data can be stored and accessed across several systems thanks to storage and integration solutions. While storage tools deal with raw data, processed data, and structured information to store it effectively and safely, integration tools are connected to the ability of data to travel across systems and applications.

Together, they provide the core of the data infrastructure that enables businesses to store, retrieve, and share data. The tools guarantee scalability and business continuity, meaning that data will always be available for analysis and operational use.

6. Tools of Governance and Security.

Governance and security tools help in ensuring that data is handled, accessed and secured as per corporate policies and legal provisions. The tools of governance would offer a control in the issues of data quality, data lineage, and metadata administration, which would grant organizations control.

Security solutions ensure that there is no access to and vulnerability of data through encryption, access, and monitoring. Combined, governance and security solutions could help ensure that company policies and procedures, and the data privacy laws are adhered to to safeguard sensitive data. over their data assets.

7. Monitoring and logging tools

The system accommodates monitoring and logging, to ensure that all the activity in the system is tracked. Monitoring and Logging Tools To trace the activity of all systems in the system, the system may provide monitoring and logging tools.

Infrastructure and pipelines Real-time pipeline and infrastructure performance and health are monitored and recorded through systems. Where logging tools can be used to have all the logs of the system activity, monitoring tools allow to view significant metrics, including system performance, as well as the rate of data flow.

The tools are useful in the detection of problems at an early stage to enable engineers to troubleshoot these problems and maximize the use of pipelines. Monitoring and logging are important in order to ensure the stability and reliability of data systems and facilitate smooth operations.

8. Data visualization and data presentation.

Reports, dashboards, graphs, and charts that display data trends, patterns, and correlations can be made by users using data visualization and presentation tools. They speed up decision-making and simplify complicated datasets by offering visual images.

Real-time data exploration and interaction are made possible by data visualization technologies. With the use of drag-and-drop interfaces found in many products, non-technical users can build visualizations without requiring a lot of coding. Additionally, these tools facilitate the integration of data from databases, spreadsheets, and cloud storage by supporting a variety of data sources.

4.1.3 Notable Tools for Data Engineering

1. Dagster

Source: (Dagster, 2026)

- **Category:** Ingestion, processing, transformation, and orchestration tools
- **Primary function:** Logging, monitoring, data transposition, and data superiority
- **License:** Apache-2.0

An open-source platform called Dagster facilitates the creation, production, and tracking of data assets over their entire development lifespan. It has best-in-class testability, integrated lineage and observability, and data validity checks, and a declarative programming language.

Key features of Dagster:

- The system allows users to build data pipelines through straightforward declarative methods which create data pipelines based on the data assets they generate.
- The system operates as your data team with its complete data tracking system which includes asset lineage and quality controls and an integrated data catalogue.
- The platform delivers managed services through its advanced CI/CD framework and its reliable managed system and ability to build custom systems.

- The system offers extensive operational links with popular data management platforms which include major cloud service providers (AWS GCP Azure) and ETL solutions (Fivetran Airbyte dlt Sling) and business intelligence applications (Tableau Power BI Looker Sigma).
- The system employs Dagster Pipes to execute any programming language code from external systems while enabling the execution of all Python-based tasks.
- The system enables you to create intelligent pipeline systems through event-driven conditions which assess both your pipeline status and upstream data assets.

2. DBT (Data Build Tool)

- **Category:** Conversion tackles
- **Main function:** Data enrichment, quality, and transformation
- **License:** Apache 2.0

"Data Build Tool" (DBT) is a SQL-first platform that uses best practices in software engineering to transform and orchestrate data pipelines. Teams can work together to create, test, and implement data conversions while preserving the integrity and governance of the data. It enables the construction of dependable, modular data pipelines by automating dependency management and supporting CI/CD workflows.

Key Features of DBT:

- **SQL-First Transformations:** The system enables users to create data transformations through SQL or Python while the system handles all dependency management and execution process.
- **Built-in Testing & Documentation:** The system maintains data reliability through its testing system which comes preconfigured and creates documentation that enhances transparency and collaborative work.

- **CI/CD & Version Control:** The system works with Git and CI/CD pipelines to provide a secure and efficient deployment process which covers development, staging, and production environments.
- **Modular & Reusable Code:** The system creates efficient operations through its reusable macros and templates which enable users to create scalable transformations that maintain uniformity.
- **Collaborative Workspace:** The system creates a unified platform which enables data science and analytics teams to work together because it supports both SQL and Python programming languages.

3. Snowflake

- **Type:** Tools for processing, transforming, storing, and integrating
- **Primary Purpose:** Security, data governance, and data integration and storage.
- **License:** Commercial

A data engineering platform called Snowflake makes it possible to handle batch and streaming data pipelines on the same platform. Its platform is cost-effective and performance-focused, allowing users to create data using declarative pipelines with Python or SQL without requiring additional infrastructure.

Key Features of Snowflake:

- **Batch pipelines and unified streaming:** Snow pipe streaming has a latency of less than 10 seconds while processing both streaming and batch data intake.
- **Dynamic tables:** To enable more effective processing, automatically maintain dependencies and materialize findings based on freshness targets.
- **Support for several languages:** Code can be executed in a single optimized engine using Python, SQL, Java, and other languages.
- **Data sharing:** Snowflake Marketplace allows live data to be accessible without the need for extra processing.

- **Intrinsic DevOps:** Programmatically deployable and manageable, it supports version control and CI/CD pipelines.

4. BigQuery

- Tools for processing, conversion, integration, and storage are categorized.
- Ingestion, batch processing, real-time processing, and data storage are the main goals.

Commercial licence

A managed serverless data warehouse called BigQuery enables effective data translation and analysis. Data engineers can swiftly run both organized and unstructured data, query, and change data using SQL and Python thanks to BigQuery's distributed and scalable architecture.

Key Features of BigQuery:

- **Serverless data warehouse:** Without the need for human provisioning, scale automatically to query terabytes of data in seconds and petabytes in minutes.
- When dealing with large-scale data workloads, separation of computation and storage improves performance and reliability by enabling storage and compute to expand separately.
- **Support for streaming and batch data:** Batch-load information from sources like files, databases, or cloud storage, or continuously ingest data with real-time streaming.
- **Advanced analytics and machine learning:** Provide ANSI SQL support, geographic analytics, and integrated machine learning with BigQuery ML.
- **Integration:** Uses federated queries to integrate using external data sources like Cloud Storage, Bigtable, and Google Sheets as well as well-known programs like Looker Studio and Tableau.

4.1.4 Data Engineering Best Practices

1. Approve a Data Products Method

Any program or instrument that analyses data and produces insights is a data product. Businesses can use these insights to improve their future decision-making. Users or customer organizations may then sell or utilize stored data, processing it as needed.

The following guidelines must be followed in order to implement a data products approach:

- Product Management Methodology, which includes the individuals and procedures responsible for creating the requirements, KPIs, and definitions.
- Suitable methods for delivering products, including all additional engineering best practices necessary to reliably provide high-quality data products
- Procedures for measurement and improvement, such as SLA agreements that include the accessibility of the interface and the freshness of the data, and ongoing observation and verification of data quality in all its facets.

2. Collaborate while Building Data Products

The situation in software engineering is extremely similar to this. Complex data product development, testing, shipping, and maintenance teams typically consist of multiple team members as well as people from other teams that use and modify the data.

In order to accomplish this, the team members must cooperate and support one another's work while maintaining their freedom to work at their own pace. To ensure that there is always a functional version available for consumption, this calls for technologies that allow the ability to continuously incorporate each other's work and safe development in a segregated setting.

3. Be Resilient with Quick Recovery from Errors

High-quality, robust items are typically not created in this manner. Even in the most seasoned teams, mistakes and bugs sometimes occur. Quick root-cause analysis, quick recovery from quality problems, and quick deployment of corrected versions are all necessary for quickly supplying high-quality data products.

In order to facilitate this, we require a system that allows us to rapidly and easily discover the root causes and test and implement a repair at the same speed. This is known as repeatability throughout testing and development.

4. Enable Continuous Delivery of Quality Data Products with CI/CD for Data

Resolving Issues with data quality in data products are important, but the only way to accomplish quick development and deployment cycles is to be able to consistently guarantee the quality of these products. By doing this, data engineers can identify and stop mistakes before they happen.

To do this, software engineers employed the concepts of hooks and pre-merge validations. By creating hooks that assess fresh data prior to it being utilized in production and prevent erroneous data from being used in production, this can and should be applied to data as well. This idea is the basis of the CI/CD methodology, which can and ought to be applied to data with the appropriate tools.

5. Leverage Data Versioning

The concept of data versioning is an important starting point that facilitates a best practice in the contemporary data management. It serves as a time machine and documents all the alterations done to data and stores it as a new version. This will further improve collaboration since each member of the team can work in their own branch or copy of the data so that the work of others is not hampered by experimentation and development. It also encourages the concept of reproducibility because the data engineers can easily rollback to an earlier version of the data in case of a mistake or failure. In addition, data versioning enhances CI/CD functions as an updated version of data is created and tested whenever data is changed. Data that is up to quality is only advanced to the main version which guarantees accuracy, reliability and confidence to the data pipeline.

• Data versioning needs an appropriate tooling – Data Version Control

In spite of the fact data versioning is an influential principle, it can really manifest itself only with the help of the appropriate tools. These provide teams with the ability to branch data and experiment in isolation, go back in time to have repeatability, and work hand in hand with CI/CD. With such capabilities, data versioning tools take the concept of data versioning and convert it into a practical and effective method to enable data engineers to control, test and deploy data in a manner that gives them confidence.

- **THE STANDARDIZED APPROACH TO VERSION CONTROL IS GIT**

Git was developed and provided version control capabilities using a common taxonomy, making it the easiest method for a data version control system. Branching, merging, and switching between versions and hooks are all simple operations made possible by the git interface.

Developers now find its "user interface" (UI) to be quite intuitive, and it is simple to include into nearly any current stack. Git for data is offered by a number of solutions, which differ in terms of features like scalability, data volume support, tabular and unstructured data support, file format compatibility, and more.

6. DESIGN EFFICIENT AND SCALABLE PIPELINES

Because they enable businesses to effectively handle the volume and complexity of data, effective data pipelines are essential for big data.

Effective pipelines ensure that data maintains its integrity, quality, and relevance while moving easily from its source to the analysis point. Teams can obtain accurate information, make wise judgements, and quickly adjust to changes in the market thanks to this.

7. AUTOMATE DATA PIPELINES AND MONITORING

The organization's ability to use the data depends on the data flowing through the pipeline. Data cleaning and repair, pipeline debugging, pipeline upgrades, drift control, ensuring the pipeline's technologies work together, and other data-related tasks overburden today's data engineers. As a result, they are forced to work long hours at boring jobs. This could have a detrimental effect on data quality.

By requiring less work to process and transmit information in the pipeline and update information columns, automation increases productivity and efficiency. Because it doesn't have to perform the data-related tasks by hand, it can operate more quickly and with less manual labour, which increases efficiency and lowers data point mistakes.

Standardization, which results from automation, is a crucial enabler of any information engineering endeavor. Errors, omissions, and drift are less likely when the pipeline transfers the same data regardless of the source and format. By improving the data's consistency, accuracy, and timeliness, this raises its quality.

Because automated data pipelines may be built to extend both horizontally and vertically to meet workload requirements and optimize resources, they are also easier to scale. Because of this, the pipeline can easily handle increasing data volumes and processing requirements without necessitating substantial reconfiguration or personal intervention.

8. Keep Data Pipelines Reliable

Think about how your data needs are changing. Evaluate your existing and future needs honestly and contrast them with the capabilities of your data processing engine and current architecture. Instead of letting antiquated technologies limit you, try to simplify things.

In your data stack, how many different services are in operation? How simple is it to get information from these services? Do obstacles between different data silos need to be overcome by your data pipelines? To accomplish adequate data protection, security, and governance, do you need to make repeated efforts or employ several data management tools? Find out which processes need an additional step (or two) and how to make them simpler. Recall that complexity poses a threat to the dependability of your data flow.

9. Avoid Data Duplicates with Idempotent Pipelines

It's a good idea to use idempotence and intelligent retries when designing your pipelines for self-healing. By responding to jobs that are unsuccessful after a set number of tries with backoff delays, try policies eliminate transient problems, including transient network failures. This guarantees that brief malfunctions won't interfere with the pipeline.

Idempotence guarantees that a procedure will yield the same outcome no matter how many times it is executed because of the retries. This is accomplished by using database transactions and the techniques of maintaining a record of processed data IDs. Combining these techniques ensures that data streams are fault-tolerant, take faults into account to a considerable extent, and prevent duplicate data from being accidentally inserted.

10. Enabling Data Sharing of Your Data Pipelines.

Effective data pipelines are based on clear and consistent documentation that transforms complex processes into shared knowledge. Each pipeline is supposed to be a tale in itself; its purpose, design, inputs, outputs, dependencies, assumptions, constraints, and performance.

In addition to this, good documentation serves as a practical guide as it provides a description of how to run, test, monitor, and troubleshoot pipelines and how to access and use the resultant data. Documentation can be made simple to navigate, manage and depend on when organized in a thought-provoking and presentable way, giving a team more control over power to work smarter and more confidently.

11. Ensure Data Quality

Correctness is not the only way that data quality is ensured within a data pipeline. It involves making data complete, uniform, reliable, and timely as it moves through collection, processing and analysis stages.

Lack of quality data may lead to wrong decisions, stagnant work and lost opportunities. As an illustration, complete data sets can create biased analytics, and regular data can cause misunderstanding and mistrust among consumers.

Moreover, timeliness which refers to the speed at which data is processed and made available to be used in making decisions is very important in the fast-paced commerce environment where real-time data is rapidly becoming the norm. The first thing to understand about data quality is that it is time to make sure that your data pipeline is not only a pipeline but a reliable source of useful business information.

12. Embrace DataOps

Managing data is not a project. to be completed every time, but it is a continuous process. It involves a continuous collection, processing and analysis of data with an aim of discovering patterns, trends and valuable insights to make informed business decisions.

The ability of companies to treat DataOps as an ongoing operation process can make them more agile and responsive to internal and external changes. This requires a culture change to a more data-driven decision-making, which includes disaggregating silos of the company and promoting teamwork among business analysts, developers, and data scientists.

The idea is to work together in order to discover needs, build pipelines, and ensure that data is accurate, timely, and relevant whichever it may be a data lake or data warehouse. In this way the organization can also develop a culture where data is seen as a strategic asset leading to better business results.

13. Focus on Business Value

Since most firms use data, data engineers are accustomed to getting their hands dirty and solving problems. They serve as the foundation for analytics and set up the pipelines and infrastructure that allow data to be sent to downstream customers without any problems. One of the main goals of data engineering is to enable an efficient data analysis. Additionally, the business outcomes increase as engineers increase learning are better.

14. Keep Records and Use correct naming convention.

Create data dictionaries and catalogues that describe the semantics and metadata of your data sources and generate data. Data dictionaries and catalogues help customers locate, understand, and trust the data generated by your pipelines. Data dictionaries and catalogues need to be maintained, searchable, interactive, and have a common terminology and structure.

15. Set Security Policy for Data

A data security policy is a reference policy that determines the manner in which organizations safeguard and handle their data resources. It defines transparent principles and guidelines in managing, storing, sharing, and accessing data and in maintaining its confidentiality, integrity, and availability. Fundamentally, the policy would help to avoid unauthorized access, misuse, or loss of data, as well as make sure that legal and regulatory standards are met. To materialize this policy, companies need to have a powerful action plan, which entails training employees, awareness creation, incorporation of security practices in normal business operations and the creation of an ongoing monitoring and enforcing of the policy- transform security into a book to a culture.

The audits and reviews are conducted regularly to determine the effectiveness of the existing controls and propose potential improvement.

4.2 ETL and ELT Data Processing Approaches

In modern data engineering, (ELT) "Extract, Load, transform" and (ETL) "Extract, Transform, Load" are two crucial techniques for preparing and modifying data for analytics and decision-making. The company must now use effective data processing techniques to ensure data quality, consistency, and usefulness due to the increasing volumes of data streaming in different directions through applications, sensors, or third-party systems.

Information is initially taken from the source systems, converted into a functional and structured format in a staging area, and then fed into a data warehouse using the traditional ETL approach. The strategy emphasizes cleaning and transforming data prior to storage; thus, it can be applied in the setting where a high level of data control and standardized schemes are required.

ELT, on the contrary, is a more recent strategy that utilizes scalability of storage systems in the form of data lakes or cloud-based data warehouses. Within this model, the information is removed and inserted into the storage system in its crude format and the transformation is performed afterwards as per the needs of analysis. This can be more flexible, is able to support both structured and unstructured data and makes the large volumes of data ingested quicker.

Whereas ETL is still applicable in the existing systems and any situation that demands high control of data, ELT has become eminent in modern data architecture, owing to its scalability, flexibility and compatibility with the current data engineering trends.

4.2.1 Difference Between ETL and ELT Processes

1. ETL process

ETL has three steps:

- You gather unprocessed data from multiple sources.
- To change that data, you employ a secondary processing server.
- You transfer that information to a target database.

The transform stage makes sure that it is in line with the structural requirements of the target database. You just transfer the data after transformation and preparation.

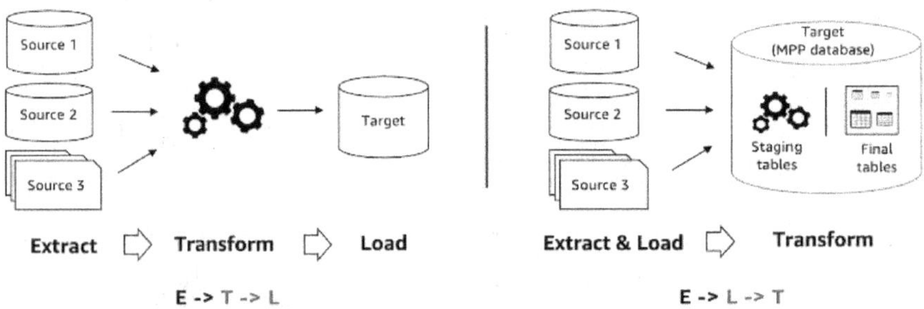

Figure 4.2: ETL vs ELT

2. ELT process

These are the three steps of ELT:

- You gather unprocessed data from multiple sources.
- You load it into a data lake or warehouse in its natural condition.
- In the target system, you modify it as necessary.

With ELT, the data warehouse is where Every step of data transformation, enrichment, and cleansing is completed. The unprocessed data can be manipulated and altered as often as necessary.

4.2.2 Key differences: ETL vs. ELT

"Extract, load, and transform" (ELT) have improved "extract, transform, and load" (ETL) in several ways.

- **Transform and load location**

Load and transformation use dissimilar processes and take place in separate places. On a secondary processing server, the ETL procedure modifies data.

The ELT method, on the other hand, imports raw data directly into the intended data warehouse. After arriving, the data can be transformed at any time.

- **Data compatibility**

ETL works best with structured data that can be shown in tables with rows and columns. It converts a set of structured data into another structured format before loading it.

ELT, on the other hand, manages all kinds of data, including unstructured data that cannot be stored in tabular form, such as papers or photos. The method loads the several data types into the target data warehouse using ELT. It can then be further transformed into the format you need.

- **Speed**

ETL is slower than ELT. Before loading data into the target, ETL has an extra phase that is hard to scale and slows down the system as the amount of data grows.

ELT, on the other hand, imports data straight into the destination system and processes it concurrently. It provides data transformation for analytics in real-time or almost real-time by utilizing the processing capacity and parallelization provided by cloud data warehouses.

- **Costs**

ETL is slower than ELT. Before loading data into the target, ETL has an extra phase It is difficult to scale and causes the system to lag as data volume increases.

ELT, on the other hand, imports data straight into the destination system and processes it concurrently. It provides real-time or almost real-time analytics data transformation using the processing capacity and parallelization provided by cloud data warehouses.

- **Security**

Data privacy laws must be followed when working with personal data. Businesses should take precautions to prevent unauthorized access to "personally identifiable information" (PII).

Developers are compelled to provide some of their own solutions in ETL, such as masking PII to track and protect data.

However, ELT systems offer numerous security features right within the data warehouse, such as multifactor authentication and granular access control. You can spend less time adhering to data regulations and more time on analytics.

4.2.3 When to use ETL vs. ELT

For contemporary analytics, "extract, load, and transform" (ELT) is the default option. But in the following situations, you might think of extracting, transforming, and loading ETL.

- **Legacy databases**

Using Integrating ETL with external data sources or legacy databases that have preset data formats can occasionally be more advantageous. It simply needs to be transformed and loaded into your system once. You can use it more effectively for all upcoming analytics once it has been converted.

- **Experimentation**

Data engineers carry out experiments in huge organizations, such as finding hidden data sources for analytics and experimenting with novel concepts to address business questions. In data studies, ETL helps understand the database and its applicability in a certain situation.

- **Complex analytics**

For complicated analytics that employ several data formats from several sources, ETL and ELT can be utilized in tandem. For some sources, data scientists may put up ETL pipelines and employ ELT for the other sources. In certain situations, this boosts application performance and enhances analytics efficiency.

- **IoT APPLICATIONS**

ETL is frequently superior to ELT for Sensor data streams are used in Internet of Things (IoT) applications. Typical use cases for ETL at the edge include the following:

- o You want to receive data from several protocols and convert it into standard data formats for usage in cloud workloads.
- o You wish to load average or filtered values at a slower rate after filtering high-frequency data and performing averaging operations on huge datasets.
- o On the local device, you wish to compute values from several data sources and transmit values that have been filtered to the cloud backend.
- o You wish to fill in the gaps in time series data, tidy up, or eliminate duplicates.

4.3 Data Ingestion and Integration Techniques

In modern data-driven organizations, maintaining a competitive edge requires the capacity to gather, process, and analyze massive amounts of data advantage. The modern business environment is characterized by the massive amount of data being followed by the business throughout the customer lifecycle and effective data management is becoming a major necessity. Two basic processes that lie at the heart of this data ecosystem are data ingestion and data integration processes, which perform different tasks when turning raw data into meaningful insights.

Data ingestion can be described as the act of gathering and bringing into a system the data of various sources to be processed further. Data integration, on the contrary, involves the incorporation and formatting of information on the various sources into one and coherent view that could be analyzed and utilized in decision-making. These processes, as much as they are an inseparable combination and they cannot be undertaken without the other, it is essential to comprehend the differences between the two processes to ensure the relevance and applicability of data.

The growing volumes of data are becoming a major challenge to maintenance of data quality during the ingestion and integration stages because the organisations continue to handle these large quantities of data. Modern tools, such as AI, which can enable organizations make more qualified and reliable decisions are also assisting to identify anomalies and data reliability as a possible solution.

4.3.1 Data Ingestion: The Foundation of Data Pipelines

Data input is the most important initial step in any data pipeline since all the rest of the data processing and analysis depend on it. It entails gathering as well as importing data in diverse sources into a system to enable its processing, examination and storage. This stage is very important because it defines the quantity and quality of data available to be utilized in the downstream activity.

The ways of data ingestion may be numerous, depending on the character of the data sources and the business requirements:

1. **Batch loading**: It is the method of collecting and loading data regularly. It comes in particularly handy when crunching data that are in high volumes but do not require real time updates. As an example, a retail company can process its sales database on a nightly basis with the help of batch ingestion.
2. **Streaming ingestion:** Data can be used to process a batch operation and streaming ingestion However, unlike Data, it cannot be used to update data in real-time, that is, it must process it as it arrives. The latter strategy is central to guiding applications that require real-time data processing, which may be a system that detects and prevents fraud or a real-time analytics dashboard.
3. **APIs (Application Programming Interfaces):** APIs allow a more complex and flexible method of data entry. They help in communication between various systems and exchange of information and this occurs efficiently and, in a need, based manner which makes them ideal where data has to be pulled off various external services or sources of data.

Even though the consumption of the data is elementary towards the construction of robust data pipelines, it is challenging. Massive data will impose a pressure on the resources of the system and require careful planning to be scalable. Handling different data formats provided by different sources may introduce more processing with strong data verification. Furthermore, the dependability and safety of the ingestion process is the most important consideration, particularly when handling sensitive data or a system that has a high level of mission critical information.

In order to solve this problem and make ingestion seamless, it is recommended that organizations follow a number of best practices:

- Use extensive data validation on source to identify and rectify faults early in the pipeline.
- Architecture ingestion processes to be scalable so that the increasing data volumes can be accommodated easily.
- Put in place elaborate monitoring mechanisms that will help in the identification and correction of any mistakes or bottlenecks in the ingestion process in the quickest time.
- Data security Take priority and introduce audit trails, encryption, and access controls throughout the intake process.

Organizations may build a solid foundation through appropriate data ingestion procedures, which will help them succeed in data integration and analysis and, eventually, make better decisions and grow their businesses.

4.3.2 Data Integration: Combining Data from Multiple Sources

In order to analyze and make decisions, data integration methods involve combining and organizing information from several systems into a single unit. This crucial step in the data pipeline transforms heterogeneous and unprocessed data into a single, valuable commodity that can be used to promote business intelligence and planning.

The commonest modes of integrating data are as follows:

- **ETL (Extract, Transform, Load):** It is a more traditional approach, where the information is taken out of different systems and then transformed to the required form or structure and then inserted into the desired system (which can be a data warehouse among others). ETL can be especially handy when transformation between systems is complex or a target system requires a particular format of data.

- **ELT (Extract, Load, Transform):** It is a more current method that inverts the steps. Once the data is extracted out of the source systems it is put into the target system in its raw form. The late transformations are created in a data lake or a warehouse. Overall, this approach is more adaptable and could utilize the processing capability of the current data storage platforms.

The problems involved in data integration do exist. They are to ensure that there is data consistency among the different sources, formatting, ensure the data between the old systems and the new data structures is maintained and reconciled, and the integrity of the data is also always upheld through the integration process. Besides this, time sensitive applications could need overhead on top of real time integration.

In order to resolve them, and make the data integration process the most efficient, the companies should be attentive to the following best practices:

- Establishing strong data mapping that will help in proper translation of various data models.
- Repetitive tasks, which are meant to be eradicated through automation to enhance efficiency.
- Adoption of data governance structures in a bid to ensure data quality and consistency.
- Improving data discoverability and understanding using metadata management.
- Periodical auditing and updating of integration processes to make them relevant to changing business requirements.

Through an effective amalgamation of data sources and integrators, one can obtain a full picture of their operations, customers and market trends and make better decisions and strategizing.

4.3.3 Key Differences Between Data Ingestion and Data Integration

Although both data integration and data ingestion are essential components of the data pipeline, their applications differ and occur at distinct times. To create successful data management methods, it is critical to comprehend these distinctions.

Aspect	Data Ingestion	Data Integration
Process	emphasizes collecting and importing raw data from multiple sources.	creates a coherent view by combining and refining data from various sources.
Stage in Data Pipeline	takes place at the pipeline's start.	usually occurs following the ingestion of data.
Goal	guarantees that data is accessible for processing	guarantees that data is appropriate for investigation and decision-making.
Scope	focuses on specific data sources	operates with several data sources
Output	Unprocessed or hardly managed data	Harmonized, organized data that is prepared for analysis

Source: (Anomalo, 2024)

Data integration and ingestion are complementary, notwithstanding their differences:

Raw data is ingested into systems which gives raw data the input required to undergo further processing. This data is ingested and improves into a format that can be analyzed by data integration. Collectively, the two make sure data is not merely present but also useful and practical in terms of business insights.

Both processes are critical towards ensuring that the data remains high quality and that it is useable in making decisions. Effective ingestion can make all the relevant data to be captured and successful integration can make this information is helpful since it provides a cohesive and consistent picture of the company.

4.4 Monitoring and Managing Data Pipelines

Data pipeline monitoring can be explained as a practice of guaranteeing the integrity and reliability of the data within the different phases of the process through the stages of ingestion and transformation, storage, and final usage.

Conventionally, most teams have been reactive in the way they monitor, and only resolved issues of data quality once they have created disturbances in the downstream.

Nevertheless, with a left-shift in monitoring, i.e. an upward displacement in the data monitoring, teams can actively identify problems prior to impacting reports, dashboards, or decision-making. This will reduce the number of interruptions and guarantee the quality of data at the earliest stages of the pipeline.

Key Takeaways

A data pipeline consists of procedures that will automate the movement, manipulation, and distribution of data across multiple sources to the location where it can be analyzed and used.

- Real-time analytics require efficient data pipelines, which allow a business to make timely and informed choices.
- Data pipelines process and analyze unstructured as well as structured data, which necessitate different methods of processing and analysis.

The construction of a data pipeline entails finer details, including data sources, processing engines and they are in unison to support the flow of data.

- Cloud services can be used to reference advanced solutions to create and operate data pipelines, open data analytics to all businesses, regardless of their sizes.

4.4.1 Classes of Data Pipeline Optimism.

The health of the data pipeline has a direct influence on the business operations.

When pipelines flow smoothly, timely and correct information is received by the decision-makers. When they fail to do so, the repercussions will be felt in your organization.

Thus in case of pipelines rupture, they not only frustrate engineers but also stump decisions.

You need to be cautious of 4 types of data pipelines.

1. Data quality issues

When data in your pipelines is inaccurate, lacking, inconsistent, or falls short of expectations, it can lead to issues with data quality.

Using a hospital network as an example, let's say that data that is fed into a pipeline gets corrupted with patient scheduling information.

Available appearance slots can be booked when the slot is in fact booked, resulting in double-bookings and frustrated patients and possible delayed care.

It does not only have financial implications, since it affects the immediate costs of operation, but also the harm on patient satisfaction scores and risks to regulatory compliance.

2. Schema drift

Schema points happen when the form of your information shifts out of control. Schema drifts may be the change of field names, type, order of fields or the addition or deletion of fields.

In more specific terms, when a CRM system used by your marketing department has been updated and now has new customer preference fields, then your current pipeline will be unaware of how to manage this new data format.

Consequently, the insights on critical customers are dropped, and your personalization algorithms have to do with incomplete information at the cost of campaign efficacy.

3. Data freshness problems

Freshness of data is also an element in the quality of data; the issue of age can lead to issues. Failure to update your data on a regular basis will affect your data pipeline and will not be able to make timely decisions or operations.

As an illustration, the inventory management system of a retail chain is based on the fresh sales information to prompt a restocking order.

When the pipeline supplying such information is slow, the stores may run out of the in-demand products in the high-shifting seasons and at the same time do excessive ordering of the slow-moving products.

4. Pipeline failures

These occur when a information duct malfunctions or halts, and the information cannot pass over the intended location.

Take the case of a financial services corporation whose financial pipeline to assess the risk malfunctions during the market hours.

In the absence of real time risk calculations then the trading decision is a blind bet and this can cost the organization in terms of millions of dollars in losses that are unforeseen in the turbulent market environment.

4.4.2 How to Monitor the Data Pipelines

A strategic approach that strikes a balance between technical control and business awareness is necessary for effective data pipeline monitoring.

It is aimed at preventing hindrances before they touch the business and not necessarily to discover mistakes once they have been made.

Integrate proactive warning initially.

Based on the nature of the issues, smart alarm systems should inform the relevant teams even before minor issues escalate into bigger problems. The monitoring technologies ought to detect abnormalities and be able to automatically respond in real time rather than rely on end users to report anomalies in the form of missing or late data.

The next step is integration of business context. The best method of monitoring ties performance and business performance to each other, beyond technical measures.

An example is that time to customer insight delivery or financial reporting lateness will be tracked in teams instead of data processing latency only.

You can be fully visible through multi-layer monitoring, whereby you will have to watch all the actions of the data flow.

This is an all-purpose method that enables teams to find issues fast and assess their downstream impacts.

Remember to use automated recovery; it can drastically cut down on manual intervention and downtime.

An efficient monitoring system can immediately restart unsuccessful jobs or switch to backup data sources when typical problems occur, such as a momentarily unavailable data source, maintaining operations seamless and uninterrupted.

4.4.3 Metrics in Pipeline Monitoring

You may acquire a competitive edge and understand what to measure by using these four key measures.

1. Traffic: Tracks how much data is flowing and where.

For instance, a manufacturing organization may monitor how many sensor readings are handled by factory machinery per hour. Unexpected increases could suggest the need for more processing power, while sudden decreases could indicate equipment faults.

2. Errors: Tracks the frequency and type of pipeline errors.

In addition to knowing that data processing failed, a telecom company keeping an eye on customer service interactions would want to know if the failure had an impact on customer satisfaction ratings, service quality measures, or billing accuracy.

3. Latency: This is the duration of time taken by the data to pass through the system.

To illustrate, it is necessary to monitor the difference between updates in shipment state and delivery of customer notification directly affect customer satisfaction and efficiency in the operation of a logistics company.

4. Saturation: Measures system capacity and bottlenecks.

It is the responsibility of a media streaming service to ensure that its content recommendation pipelines will be able to handle peak viewing times without degrading performance or not making customized recommendations.

4.4.4 Data Pipeline Monitoring Dashboard

A data pipeline monitoring dashboard is your command center of data health in your company. It is a centralized view that transforms computations that are complex technically to helpful business insights. The dashboard must contain information about your data infrastructure and display it in a manner that will be easy to turn into prompt decisions.

An effective visualisation indicates what is important: Are our pipelines serving business purposes? This does away with the business leaders having to examine raw technical records.

These dashboards can be used by data engineers as well as other people. Various team members use monitoring dashboards towards different purposes.

Business analysts are preoccupied with the indicators of quality and the fresher data that influences their reports, whereas data engineers are focused on the technical performance metrics and removal of errors. Executive leadership on the other hand would pursue business impact summaries and high-level health indicators. Dashboard in particular can be of great use in incident response since it is easier to quickly locate the affected pipelines and understand the business impact and organize the response activities in case of problems without the need to switch between interfaces.

With the absence of centralized nursing, companies do not know the health of their data infrastructure until problems manifest themselves in the form of disruption to the business processes. By the time the customer-facing apps manifest false information or revenue indication reports display inconsistency, the damage is already done.

There are five vital components of your dashboard, including:

- **Live status indicators:** These are graphical representations of the approximate pipeline fitness that represent a system status in real-time in a manner similar to traffic lights.
- **Business effect measures:** KPIs relating business results to technical results, e.g. freshness of revenue reporting or the percentage of accurate customer data.

- **Historical trend analysis:** The long-term dependability trends, the capacity planning needs and the seasonal variations can be calculated using diagrams and charts that show performance trends with time.
- **Alert management interface**: This allows for coordinated incident management by providing a centralized view of current alerts, their response status, and their priority levels.
- **Resource utilization** monitors assist teams in determining when scaling is required by providing both historical and real-time views of infrastructure capacity.

4.4.5 Data Pipeline Monitoring Dashboard Example

Suppose Med Advance Therapeutics, a fictional pharmaceutical research firm, chooses to make use of its data pipeline monitoring dashboard to handle the processing of clinical trial data.

Med Advance is a company with several parallel clinical trials in various clinical areas.

Every study generates enormous amounts of patient data, lab results, and adverse event reports that must be handled, vetted, and made available to research teams within stringent regulatory time limits.

The six major sections shown in their monitoring dashboard include:

- **Trial data ingestion status**

Displays the real-time processing status of all trial sites that are active.

Normal processing results in green indicators, minor delays are recorded in yellow indicators and critical issues are highlighted by red flags and need to be addressed first.

- **Measures of regulatory compliance.**

Check the timeframes of monitors data processing in relation to FDA regulations.

A high and bright counter would show the number of days to the regulatory submission deadline of each phase of the trial, and the health of the pipeline would be linked directly to the achievement of these critical deadlines.

- **Data quality scorecard**

Presents patient records, lab results and safety report completeness and accuracy measures.

The dashboard also alerts when the data quality scores make less than the acceptable levels and this could affect the validity of the trials.

- **Resource utilization panel**

Calculates and reports usage of computers and storage materials in the processing of data.

This is useful when the team anticipates a peak in trial enrolment, and will purposely increase possessions before presentation suffers.

- **Alert summary**

Business impact priorities Lists lively subjects sorted by commercial influence.

As an illustration, a Trial XYZ-001 Lab result processing delay will have a high priority since it influences a Phase III trial that is about to be completed.

- **Trends of historical performance.**

Figure illustrating the results of the performance of the pipes within the last few months that assists in defining a pattern and strategizing on the next milestones of the trial.

- **Business Impact**

Med Advance was able to improve regulatory submission accuracy, avoid potential delays, and reduce trial data processing time by 60% thanks to this dashboard which might have cost millions of dollars in prolonged trial time.

4.4.6 Features in Data Pipeline Monitoring Tools

You shouldn't overlook the following elements when selecting your data pipeline monitoring tool:

- **Data quality monitoring**

Data consistency, accuracy, and completeness are continuously evaluated.

For instance, keeping an eye on client information to make sure phone numbers have the right number of digits and email addresses are formatted correctly.

- **Schema evolution tracking**

Data structure changes are automatically detected, and impact analysis indicates which downstream processes may be impacted.

- **Lineage visualization**

Interactive maps that illustrate the data flow within your company make it simpler to comprehend dependencies and identify the root of problems.

- **Performance optimization**

Bottlenecks and resource limitations that impact pipeline performance are identified, along with suggestions for improvement.

- **Collaboration features**

Tools that make it possible for executives, business analysts, and data teams to coordinate solutions to data problems and exchange ideas.

4.5 Workflow Orchestration and Automation

Workflow orchestration involves coordinating automated tasks throughout business applications and services to achieve complete operational efficiency.

The goal of workflow automation is to automate specific operations. On the other hand, workflow orchestration establishes a unified system which enables automated tasks to function together as they move through their operational sequence while connecting with other systems to complete a business operation. Successful workflow orchestration achieves operational efficiency by managing tasks which include data processing, system upgrades, notifications, and approvals.

Modern orchestration systems make use of software programs and workflow orchestration platforms that incorporate low-code tools, artificial intelligence, and machine learning as their core technology. The technologies enable users to create workflows which run without interruptions while preserving their original design through an automated process which generates predefined tasks and connects to outside systems, such as cloud services, enterprise resource planning, and customer relationship management.

Workflow orchestration systems can now operate with more autonomous functionality thanks to the use of agentic AI. The ability of these models to behave autonomously, make decisions, start workflows, and modify procedures on the fly without continual human interaction is referred to as "agentic."

Workflow orchestration gives businesses the ability to monitor process performance because it allows them to observe their workflows in real time. The system enables organizations to find workflow bottlenecks and make operational changes based on data analysis. The system provides workflow orchestration capabilities to businesses which need to handle their expanding operational procedures while they scale their operations.

4.5.1 Importance of Workflow Orchestration

Organizations depend on multiple applications and technologies to execute their various operational tasks. The process of workflow organization allows teams to coordinate their complex work activities through multiple tools and systems and different organizational units. The system enables multiple applications to function together by automating task performance and controlling task dependencies.

The system allows users to see all operations while they can track processes in real time. The organization uses this oversight to discover problems while it sustains its operational efficiency and fulfills its legal obligations. Workflow orchestration enables businesses to expand their operations by linking data pipelines from various sources and promoting cooperation between different departments.

Digital transformation requires workflow orchestration as its core component. The system increases efficiency through automated execution of standard operations while it ensures uninterrupted performance of critical business functions which include customer onboarding and supply chain management and IT operations. The system improves business results through its capacity to decrease manual tasks and its ability to provide dependable performance.

4.5.2 Comparison of Workflow Orchestration with Similar Practices

People often confuse workflow orchestration with other processes which include workflow automation, data orchestration, and process orchestration. Here is a brief description of each:

Workflow orchestration the system handles management and coordination tasks which connect multiple tasks and systems and tools to produce a defined result. The system enables complete workflow execution throughout various environments while maintaining task sequence and dependency requirements.

- **Workflow automation** the process of using technology for task execution needs only reduced human participation. The system enables users to automate single tasks but the functionality of workflow orchestration remains beyond its capabilities. The automated tasks of a system require workflow orchestration to handle their execution order and operational flow between different tasks.
- **Data orchestration** the research investigates systems which handle data movement together with data transformation and data integration through extract transform load processes and data lake implementation. Its main goal is to enhance workflows and decision-making processes by ensuring that data moves accurately and smoothly between sources, storage, and applications.

- **Process orchestration** the process involves overseeing multiple business operations which require both employee and system management together with workflow handling. The system extends beyond workflow orchestration because it manages complete business operations from start to finish while ensuring all activities match company objectives.

4.5.3 Workflow orchestration steps

Successful workflow orchestration often includes these steps:

- o Define objectives
- o Design the workflow structure
- o Select tools and technologies
- o Implement and integrate
- o Define monitoring and error handling
- o Test and validate workflows
- o Deploy and optimize

- **Define objectives**

Identify key tasks, dependencies and expected results. Recognize the inefficiencies in the existing method, and thereby define what areas would benefit from automation and optimization.

- **Design the workflow structure**

You need to create a detailed workflow that defines task sequences between related tasks and decision points. The current stage of the project requires the development of visual tools through process diagrams and directed acyclic graphs to establish logical flow and execution clarity.

- **Selecting tools and technologies**

Successful automation requires organizations to select appropriate orchestration tools for their automation needs. organizations use cloud platforms together with open-source platforms to achieve effective workflow management through their API integrations and database connections which enable smooth system communication. The procedure of choosing is dependent on scalability requirements, infrastructure compatibility, as well as, the workflow complexity. Many of these teams use Python scripts to write custom connectors in order to automate task logic in their orchestration frameworks.

- **Implement and Integrate**

Once implementing the design and tools, automated task execution using scripts and APIs and event-driven triggers should be used. This involves establishing connections among different applications and systems so that data can flow seamlessly within the systems.

- **Define Error Handling and Monitoring.**

To monitor performance problems, the system must have real-time monitoring to monitor its implementation and identify any failures. The organization must put in place logging systems as well as alert systems that will notify the teams about any problem in the system. Automated recovery will be employed by the system to include fallback procedures and retries so that operational stability is achieved.

- **Test and Validate Workflows**

The testing procedure must identify all the errors and inefficiencies in the system and other operational misconfigurations prior to the entire system implementation. The testing process will involve test cases to confirm proper dependency management and proper functionality of the automation system. During this stage, performance analysis aids in improving execution sequencing for optimal effectiveness.

- **Deploy and Optimize**

The team needs to monitor the live workflow which requires them to do continuous performance tests and optimization work to ensure operational effectiveness. The analysis of execution data helps to improve resource distribution and automation procedures which leads to better system performance. The organization achieves better results through ongoing improvements which help the workflow system to adapt to new business requirements and technological progress. The orchestration process effectively manages all stages of the workflow from its first deployment to the final phase of monitoring and scaling and retiring the system.

4.5.4 Workflow orchestration benefits

Workflow orchestration provides several key benefits that improve business operations.

- **Increased efficiency:** Workflow orchestration enables teams to create and deploy and track their work through its automated management of intricate processes. The system boosts operational efficiency by executing tasks that would require engineers too much time to complete through their own manual work or their sporadic task handling.
- **Improved reliability:** Workflow orchestration lowers the possibility of errors and improves process reliability by managing dependencies between jobs and ensuring that they are completed in the proper order.
- **Enhanced observability:** The workflow orchestration system achieves complete workflow visibility because it tracks every task from initiation to completion while allowing users to monitor progress and initiate retries.
- **Scalability:** The system enables your organization to handle increased demand without decreasing performance or accuracy through its scalable workflow orchestration capabilities.
- **Adaptability:** The workflow orchestration system provides organizations with multiple trigger and infrastructure options which support their needs for different operational scenarios and evolving business requirements.

4.5.5 Working of workflow automation

Task management software is used in workflow automation to route information and tasks between individuals and systems according to preset triggers and criteria. The automation system saves time and reduces errors because it sends completed tasks to the next assignee while updating dashboards.

The following steps are mentioned below

- The project needs to collect information about team task progression and current team member duties to assess the existing work process. The study should focus on three main areas which include project initiation processes and task completion criteria and work boundaries and process bottleneck development. The project team needs to identify all events which lead to task initiation and task modification.

- The visual representation of the workflow process helps to detect operational problems. The development of a draft workflow outline will help to demonstrate points where the process fails. The draft document should be improved through cross-functional team work which will also help to identify processes that waste resources.
- The identification process needs to find all tasks which demand data from external systems while verifying that the workflow software can handle these requirements. The workflow needs to be modified to establish integration requirements which include breaking down tasks into multiple smaller components.
- Take care of workflow inefficiencies, such as delayed tasks and poor communication. The solution requires development of task accountability systems together with definition of system information flow requirements.
- Workflow automation software enables users to describe tasks while developers establish user permissions. The project team needs access to Gantt charts and process maps and calendars according to project scope requirements.
- The system enables users to establish automated triggers which initiate predefined actions for their repetitive work activities. Users can create customized automation recipes according to their specific needs or choose from the available pre-designed options.
- Automated workflow testing needs ongoing optimization work to solve existing problems. Efficiency requires the establishment of performance measurements and key performance indicators monitoring purposes. The team uses dashboards to track progress and identify obstacles which need resolution.
- The team needs training on the new automated workflow system through practical demonstration sessions. The team needs change management plans to help them adapt to process modifications and upcoming workflow improvements.

MULTIPLE CHOICE QUESTIONS (MCQs)

1. **Which of the following best describes modern data engineering?**
   A. Manual collection and storage of paper records
   B. Designing, building, and maintaining scalable data systems
   C. Only creating dashboards for business users
   D. Writing reports without data validation
2. **What is the main difference between ETL and ELT?**
   A. ETL loads data before transformation, while ELT transforms before loading
   B. ETL transforms data before loading, while ELT loads data before transformation
   C. ETL is only used in cloud systems, while ELT is used on-premises
   D. There is no difference between ETL and ELT
3. **Which of the following is a common data ingestion technique?**
   A. Data archiving
   B. Batch and streaming ingestion
   C. File compression only
   D. Manual note-taking
4. **Why is workflow orchestration important in data pipelines?**
   A. It increases hardware costs
   B. It replaces the need for data validation
   C. It automates and coordinates pipeline tasks efficiently
   D. It stores data permanently
5. **Which of the following is a key goal of monitoring data pipelines?**
   A. To increase duplicate records
   B. To detect failures, delays, and performance issues
   C. To remove all historical data
   D. To avoid automation

6. In a modern cloud-based data architecture, ELT is often preferred because:

A. It avoids storing raw data

B. Cloud platforms provide scalable compute for transformations

C. It does not require automation

D. It eliminates the need for integration

7. Which of the following tools is commonly associated with workflow orchestration?

A. Microsoft Paint

B. Apache Airflow

C. Adobe Photoshop

D. VLC Media Player

8. What is the primary purpose of data integration in a pipeline?

A. To delete data from all sources

B. To combine data from multiple sources into a unified format

C. To convert all data into images

D. To reduce storage by removing metadata only

9. Which metric is most useful for evaluating the health of a data pipeline?

A. Screen brightness

B. Number of fonts used in reports

C. Pipeline execution success rate

D. Keyboard typing speed

10. Automation in data pipelines primarily helps to:

A. Increase manual intervention

B. Reduce consistency in processing

C. Improve efficiency, repeatability, and reliability

D. Prevent data collection

Answers

1	2	3	4	5	6	7	8	9	10
B	B	B	C	B	B	B	B	C	C

Chapter 5

Future Trends in Data Platforms

5.1 Serverless Data Platforms

Serverless Data platforms can be described as cloud-based solutions that can store, process, and analyze data without the need of the user to maintain server infrastructure. In traditional data architectures, provisioning, maintaining, and scaling of servers are the responsibilities of the organization to manage workloads. Serverless platforms in contrast decouple these capabilities, users only think about data operations like querying, transformation, and analytics. These capabilities are provided by fully managed services by cloud service providers such as Microsoft Azure, Google Cloud, and Amazon Web Services (Assunção et al., 2015).

The main feature of serverless data platforms is their scale-on-demand and pay-as-you-use pricing structure. The allocation and modification of resources is also done automatically according to the workload requirements without requiring any labor. Billing is done according to the real data processed or the computer resources used, instead of the capacity allocated. Examples of this strategy include AWS Lambda, Google BigQuery and Azure Synapse Analytics, which provide the ability to run on-demand and scale data warehousing.

Serverless data platforms are commonly used in the current data engineering processes, such as data ingestion, transformation, and real-time analytics. These platforms will be integrated with different sources of data and will facilitate automated pipelines, which are efficient to process large and diverse data. They are also flexible and hence can be used in applications where the workload varies or is unpredictable since the system can easily scale up smoothly without prior capacity planning. This decreases the complexity of operations, and it increases the speed at which solutions based on the data are formed.

Serverless data platforms, though they have their benefits, have a few limitations. These can be latency due to cold starts, less ability to control infrastructure setups, and even inefficient use of cost to maintain high workloads. Additionally, debugging and performance optimization can be more challenging due to the abstracted nature of the environment. Nevertheless, serverless data platforms continuing to have a major impact in modern data architectures by offering a balance of scalability, efficiency, and ease of use.

5.1.1 Understanding Serverless Ecosystem

- **Serverless and FaaS**

"Function as a service" (FaaS) is a cloud computing service that allows developers to run code or containers in response to certain events or requests without having to define or maintain the infrastructure required to run the code only one aspect of serverless computing.

The compute model at the heart of serverless computing is called FaaS, and the phrases are frequently used synonymously. In contrast to FaaS, serverless refers to a whole stack of services that can react to particular requests or events and scale to zero when not in use. The cloud provider is in charge of provisioning, management, and payment for these services, which developers cannot see.

These services include event-driven architecture, databases, storage, and gateways for application programming interfaces (APIs) in addition to FaaS.

- **Serverless databases and storage**

The data layer is built on databases (SQL and NoSQL) and storage, especially object storage. In order to adopt a serverless approach to these technologies, "instances" with fixed capacity, connection, and query limits must be replaced with models that expand linearly with infrastructure and price demand.

- **API GATEWAYS**

In addition to providing API gateways, which feature HTTP method routing, client ID and secrets, rate constraints, CORS, watching API usage, reading response logs, and API sharing regulations, serve as proxies for web application actions.

- **SERVERLESS AND EVENT-DRIVEN ARCHITECTURE**

Workloads that are event-driven and stream-processing, such as the open-source Apache Kafka event streaming platform, greatly benefit from serverless architectures.

The purpose of stateless automated serverless procedures is to handle individual instances. These characteristics are currently crucial to "event-driven architecture" (EDA), a paradigm for software design that emphasises event publication, capture, processing, and storage. Event producers, including microservices, APIs, and IoT devices, send real-time event alerts to event consumers in an EDA framework, initiating particular processing steps. For instance, when Netflix releases a new original series, several EDA services are awaiting the release news series, which sets off a sequence of updates to notify viewers. Event-driven architecture is used by numerous other businesses that develop user-facing online and mobile applications.

5.1.2 FUNDAMENTAL CAPABILITIES OF SERVERLESS SYSTEMS

Organisations can benefit from the serverless paradigm in a number of ways. In contrast to traditional server computer models, serverless computing is:

- **Maintenance-free:** Patching, updating, capacity management, performance optimisation, and other infrastructure administration issues are no longer a concern for teams. Developers can concentrate on creating code to address client issues.
- **Cost-Effective and Efficient:** In order to ensure that resources are available when needed without teams overprovisioning or paying for unnecessary resources, serverless solutions automatically modify infrastructure in response to demand.
- **Scalable and available:** An elastic environment that is instantaneously available and automatically scales without human intervention is offered by serverless compute.

- **Reliable:** Serverless compute uses server pools with automatic recovery to reduce downtime at the cloud service provider level.
- **Simplified backend code:** FaaS enables programmers to design basic functions that carry out a certain operation on their own, like contacting an API.
- **Quicker turnaround:** Time to market can be greatly reduced using serverless architecture. Developers can add and change code piecemeal rather than requiring a complex deployment process to distribute bug fixes and new features.

Instead, then concentrating on regular infrastructure, serverless enables businesses to concentrate on high-value tasks like reacting to customer input and promptly delivering code changes. This helps businesses stay competitive and launch products more quickly.

5.1.3 Pros and Cons of serverless

Pros:

There are several technical and financial advantages to serverless computing for both individual developers and business development teams:

- **Enhanced productivity among developers**: Serverless removes the infrastructure overhead on developers, who can write and even refine code. It gives the development teams more space and time to work on powerful business logic and design front end features that are captivating.
- **Pay as you drive:** Serverless implies that you only pay based on the actual consumption. The payment of the bill is instant upon the activation of an order until the time it is executed. Unlike the IaaS model where the cost is billed between the process of provisioning and decommissioning of the resources, serverless offers cost efficiency and effective utilization.
- **Speak any language:** Serverless is a polyglot and highly adaptable place, in which a developer can code in his language of choice. It may be Python, JavaScript, Java, or even Node.js, that is, it is not important to which app developers feel comfortable to work, it is safe to say that they can design an app with tools and frameworks with which they are comfortable.

- **Easier development or DevOps:** Serverless makes the whole development process easier as infrastructure definition and management is not required. Integration and the testing of all the way to deployment are faster and simpler and enable efficient and agile DevOps practices.
- **Cost-effective operation:** Serverless computing offers excellent performance and makes sure that the price is maintained to affordable levels. It can be extremely quick and productive when compared to conventional procedures of computing in the instance of workloads like parallel computing, stream computing or data-intensive computing.
- **Lower latency:** Serverless establishes a more intense proximity between the end user and the code, decreasing delays, and increasing responsiveness. This develops a faster execution and overall better user experience.
- **Visibility of usage:** Serverless systems are visible by default by collecting and analyzing usage metrics. This gives the organizations a clear picture of the performance and activity of the system by the users to make smarter and better decisions.

Cons:

Although serverless has numerous benefits, it's important to take into account several drawbacks:

- **Less control:** In a serverless environment, a company transfers server control to a third-party CSP, giving up control over execution environments and hardware.
- **Vendor lock-in:** Every service provider has distinct serverless features and capabilities that are incompatible with those of other providers.
- **Delayed startup:** Sometimes referred to as "cold start," delayed startup might have an impact on serverless applications' responsiveness and performance, especially in real-time demand scenarios.
- **Complicated testing and debugging:** Because developers cannot see back-end operations, debugging can be more difficult when using a serverless computing approach.
- **More expensive to run lengthy applications:** Serverless execution models aren't made to run code for long stretches of time. As a result,

long-running processes may be more expensive than conventional dedicated server or virtual machine setups.

5.1.4 Serverless Use Cases

Because of Serverless architecture is ideal for use cases including microservices, mobile back-ends, and data and event stream processing because of its special characteristics and advantages.

- **Serverless and microservices**

Currently, supporting microservices architectures is the most popular use case for serverless computing. The goal of the microservices paradigm is to develop little services that carry out particular tasks and communicate with each other via APIs. Serverless gained a lot of popularity due to its advantages, which include short code, automatic and built-in scalability, quick provisioning, as well as a pricing approach that never imposes idle capacity charges, even if PaaS or containers may also be used to develop and execute microservices.

- **API backends**

Every activity (or function) in a serverless platform can be converted into an HTTP endpoint that web clients can utilise. When these actions are enabled on the web, they are called web actions. Once you have web actions, you can combine them with an API gateway to create a fully functional API with additional security, support for OAuth3, rate restriction, and support for custom domains.

- **Open Liberty InstantOn (CRIU)**

A unique method is used by Open Liberty InstantOn4 to enable quick serverless application launch. During the application build process, you can use InstantOn to Make a checkpoint of your Java application process while it's running so you can subsequently restore it in manufacturing. The restore is perfect for serverless because of its quickness (in the low 100s of milliseconds). InstantOn acts as a checkpoint for your running program, therefore it's actions—including its outstanding throughput performance—remains the same after restoration. Through this technique, businesses can implement serverless for both new cloud-native applications and existing enterprises.

- **Data processing**

Make a checkpoint of your Java application process while it's running so you can subsequently restore it in manufacturing. Because of its quickness (in the low 100s of milliseconds), the restore is perfect for serverless.

- **Massively parallel compute and "map" operations**

A serverless runtime can be effectively used for any embarrassingly parallel work, where each parallelizable task results in a single action call. Web scraping and MapReduce operations, Genomic processing, Monte Carlo simulations, business process automation, hyperparameter adjustment, and data search and processing (especially cloud object storage) are a few examples of activities.

- **Stream processing workload**

A solid basis for real-time buildouts of data pipelines and streaming applications is provided by combining managed Apache Kafka with FaaS, databases, and storage. Application log data, IoT sensor data, financial market data, and corporate data streams (from other data sources) are just a few examples of the various data stream ingestions that these architectures are perfect for working with (for validation, cleansing, enrichment, and transformation).

- **AI and serverless**

Serverless ensures maximum performance and speeds up innovation by offering the automated scalability required to run machine learning (ML) and artificial intelligence (AI) applications.

- **Serverless and hybrid cloud**

By offering the Scalability, agility, and flexibility are necessary to manage different workloads in serverless, on-premises, public, and private cloud systems. computing enables a hybrid cloud strategy.

- **Typical serverless apps**

CRM, HPC, big data analytics, digital commerce, telemedicine, gaming, video streaming, chatbots, and business process automation development, and many other popular applications are supported by serverless.

5.1.5 Challenges Addressed by Serverless Computing

Serverless computing assists businesses in resolving a number of issues brought on by traditional server computer models, such as:

- **Time-consuming management**: Businesses have long struggled with configuring and managing computing, particularly choosing the right compute type for a given workload. This takes up time that could be used for more important business objectives.
- **Expensive idle time:** Conventional server compute incurs additional expenses since businesses must pay for idle time, which includes activities like compute initialisation and scale-up, in addition to the time it takes to handle workloads.
- **Inefficiency**: Managing infrastructure by hand is frequently ineffective. Teams that employ manual approaches, for instance, could overprovision compute and wind up paying for capacity they don't use or utilise.
- **sluggish processing:** Teams may have to wait for infrastructure resources to become available to perform queries or have sluggish compute start up since compute is not always available when needed.
- **Incapacity to scale:** Infrastructure capacity cannot keep up with demand in the absence of sophisticated autoscaling. Developers must think about usage in addition to writing code.
- **Service interruption:** Systems must be designed for high resilience and fallback in the event of server failure because unplanned downtime frequently causes service interruptions.

5.2 Data Governance and Privacy Challenges

Data governance is an all-encompassing strategy that includes the guidelines, procedures, and resources required to maintain the data assets of a business over time. Data governance improves data management, quality, visibility, security, and compliance capabilities throughout the entire organization by coordinating data-related requirements with business strategy. Companies may ensure regulatory compliance, protect their data from illegal access, and make data readily available for data-driven decision-making by implementing an effective data governance policy.

In general, data privacy refers to a person's right to control how, when, and how much of their personal information is disclosed or shared with third parties. A person's name, address, phone number, and online and offline behaviors can all be considered personal information. Similar to how someone could desire to limit or stop various forms of personal data collection, many internet users would like to keep others out of a private chat.

As Internet usage has increased over time, Data privacy is now more important. In order to deliver services, websites, apps, and social media platforms frequently need to gather and store user personal data. However, users may not realize that they have less privacy because some platforms and apps may gather and use more data than they anticipate. If other apps and platforms don't sufficiently safeguard the information they gather because a data breach could jeopardize user privacy.

5.2.1 The Importance of Data privacy

Nowadays, the typical business gathers a tonne of consumer data. In order to comply with regulations, maintain a secure security posture, Organisations have a duty to safeguard this data's privacy in order to obtain a competitive advantage.

Regulatory Compliance

Data privacy is widely international organizations like Many countries have established legal frameworks to protect personal information, and the UN has recognized it as a fundamental human right. These laws impose strict standards on organizations regarding data collecting, processing, sharing, and storage. Noncompliance may result in severe financial penalties and reputational damage.

The General Data Protection Regulation, or GDPR, is one of the data protections laws. It establishes stringent rules for managing personal information and it covers any organization that handles data of people that are under its jurisdiction even though the location of the organization is not a consideration. Other regions across the globe have followed the same regulatory frameworks and this reiterates an increased global concern on data protection and privacy of users.

In various nations, the laws related to data protection are still in progress and the governments are bringing up new legislations to deal with the arising issues in the digital space. These rules usually focus on transparency, user consent, minimization of data and accountability. Companies that conduct business in various locations, thus, have to make sure they comply with the different legal regulations and data governance is becoming a rather complicated yet indispensable part of business.

- **Security Posture**

Current organizations receive and store vast amounts of sensitive/ personally identifiable data (PII) which includes financial data, identification numbers, and company/business-specific information. Such information is very desirable and is often the target of cybercriminals to commit an identity theft, scam, and resell it unlicensed.

Breach of data may lead to significant financial and operational impacts such as shut down of the system, roles taken to court and loss of customer confidence. Consequently, companies have to embrace robust cybersecurity strategies in order to protect confidential data. "Identity and access management" (IAM), threat detection systems, and encryption are some of the tools that are instrumental in risk reduction and prevention of unauthorized access.

Humans factors have an impact that is also significant to the results of security in addition to the technological solutions. The following data privacy best practices which may be exercised by employees and users reduce their exposure to cyber threats, including sharing of personal information and secure digital habits. A holistic security posture is thus a combination of technical and user engagement in ensuring that dynamic cyber threats are effectively dealt with.

- **Competitive Advantage**

Effective data privacy management is capable of giving any organization a major competitive edge in the current data-driven economy. Consumers are becoming more conscious regarding how their personal information is used and will be more willing to believe in the organizations that are transparent and accountable with their use.

Companies that value data security make it easier to establish relationships with customers on a long-term basis and increase brand awareness. On the other hand, data security breaches may result in loss of confidence, diminished customer interactions and reputation in the short term. Trust is a decisive factor nowadays, which affects decisions made by a user and business performance.

Moreover, with the increased inter-organizational data sharing, it is necessary to keep privacy in the data lifecycle. Companies usually have the duty of demanding that the 3 rd party partners and service providers follow the same standards of data protection. Proper data privacy policies and governance system help companies to use new technology, like artificial intelligence, securely and in a way that does not compromise but keeps sensitive data secure.

5.2.2 Key elements of Data governance

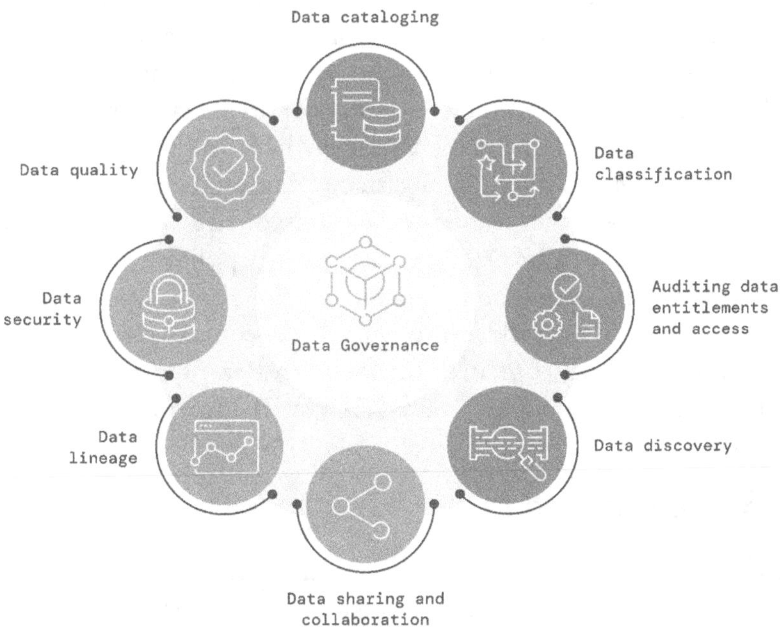

Figure 5.1: Data Governance Elements

- **Data cataloging**

To have proper data governance, one needs to be aware of the available information inside a company. A catalogue of data is where a data catalog is provided since it serves as a central repository of metadata information of data assets of an organization. A data catalog enables quick discovery, comprehension, and access to the data required by the stakeholders to enhance data-related operations, specifically analytics, governance, and discovery. It is a searchable index to all of the available data, which provides semantic meaning to an otherwise unrecognizable sea of information by providing details on the format, structure, location, and usage of the data. Organizations may be able to improve data management, foster greater collaboration, reduce redundancy, have adequate access controls, and audit information retrieval by including a data catalogue into a governance program.

- **DATA QUALITY**

Nowadays, Data quality is crucial in today's data-driven world to ensure accurate analytics, well-informed decisions, and economical outcomes. The direct impact of data quality is one of the characteristics of data governance on the credibility of decisions that are made based on data. In order to achieve a good data governance, organizations should ensure that they pay special attention to the assessment of the main data quality characteristics, which include accuracy, completeness, freshness, and adherence to data-quality regulations. Consequently, much attention to Any data governance must priorities data quality policy because it assists in tracing data lineage, implement data quality policies, as well as monitoring changes. You should not risk your business decision and resource allocation with poor data quality, but instead, focus and emphasize data quality as an important component of your data governance initiative to achieve improved results.

- **DATA CLASSIFICATION**

Intensely important in data governance is the concept that is known as data classification; in this concept, data is organized and categorized according to its criticality, worth, and sensitivity. Businesses are increasingly concerned about data security, risk mitigation, and data quality due to the unstoppable growth of data. In order to implement the appropriate security controls and policies, classification allows organizations to identify and classify data based on their level of relevance and risk. An efficient data classification system reduces risks, promotes improved data governance, and offers large-scale data quality and safety.

- **DATA SECURITY**

Businesses understand how critical it is to give their staff access to high-quality data in order to advance insights and commercial value and focus on the protection of sensitive data against unauthorized disclosure. Data security and governance heavily rely on access of data, and an ideal data security governance program must have access controls, which specify access permissions of specific groups or individuals to specific information. These controls could be highly particular to a particular record or file. With the risk of data breaches and standards like GDPR and CCPA becoming more common, companies need to create effective governance policies that specify the access of sensitive data sets by specific persons and methods of monitoring abuse. It should not be possible to access private or sensitive information unauthorized and proper control measures should be taken on access management to protect data as well as ensure that customers do not lose trust.

- **ACCESS AND DATA ENTITLEMENT AUDITING.**

Auditing of data access is a key issue in programs for Control over data governance and security, especially in regulated industries have to comply. Knowing who can access what information and how that information has been accessed lately can help organizations manually see who has been too entitled to information, and change their permissions, in turn, reducing the threat of data misuse. The absence of appropriate audit mechanisms can put an organization at the risk of not having a complete understanding of their risk surface area and are susceptible to regulatory noncompliance and data breaches. A well-designed audit team within a data governance or security governance organization is crucial to ensuring data security and compliance with regulations such as the CCPA and GDPR. By implementing effective data access auditing methodologies, organizations may protect their customers' trust and prevent misuse or unauthorized access to their data.

- **DATA LINEAGE**

By giving organizations a better awareness of data sources and consumption, data lineage is an effective tool for ensuring data quality and reliability. By documenting pertinent events and metadata at each step of the data's existence, it offers an end-to-end perspective of the data flow throughout an organization's data estate. An effective data governance framework must include data lineage helps organizations become audit-ready and compliant while lowering the operational cost of creating audit trails by hand and providing trustworthy sources for audit reports. Additionally, data lineage helps data teams and allows data consumers to perform more in-depth studies in identifying the source of any mistakes, which drastically cuts down on debugging time.

- **DATA DISCOVERY**

With organizations accumulating enormous amounts of data from various sources, it is becoming more important to make sure that this data can be found with ease to be used in scenarios involving analytics, AI, or ML. In order to offer the data its actual value and expedite data democratization, this is essential. Additionally, finding contemporary data assets including notebooks, libraries, dashboards, machine learning models, and queries has become one of the main pillars of a strong data governance strategy. Data discovery must be considered as a key element of the data governance approach of organizations. It also allows data teams to easily locate data assets inside the company, work on various initiatives, and be able to innovate swiftly and effectively. This also helps to avoid duplication of data that can be disadvantageous since it requires money to maintain them and can cause a problem of governance at various levels of security.

- **SHARING AND COOPERATION OF DATA.**

The sharing of data and collaboration is an essential part of the modern business world where organizations communicate data across many clouds, data platforms, and geographical locations with their staff, outside partners, and clients. Organizations must safely communicate data while maintaining visibility and control over how their private information is used as the need for external data keeps growing. Data cleanrooms are crucial to safe and controlled data collaboration because they guarantee that data privacy rules are upheld. Organizations must invest in open format, interoperable, and multicloud data in order to meet their needs for data-driven innovation sharing platforms. Additionally, data marketplaces facilitate the discovery and dissemination of data sets by acting as a link between customers and data suppliers. As a result, it is critical to reframe data sharing as an essential component of a strong data governance strategy and a business requirement.

5.2.3 Data Privacy Principles

An interdisciplinary team comprising members from the legal, compliance, IT, and cybersecurity departments oversees data privacy in many businesses. These organizations create data management policies that control how their companies gather, utilize, and safeguard data while taking consumers' right to privacy into consideration. They also put in place technical safeguards to protect data and create procedures for users to assert their rights.

A number of data privacy frameworks, such as the Fair Information Practice Principles and the NIST Privacy Framework1, can be used by organizations to drive their data policy. Furthermore, the privacy regulations largely determine the details of every organization's data governance policy regulation of the company must abide by, if any.

Nevertheless, most frameworks and rules contain a few general data privacy principles. The data privacy policies, procedures, and controls of many organisations are based on these concepts.

- **Access**

Users are entitled to find out what data a company possesses. Users should be able to access their personal data whenever they choose. They should be allowed to update or change such information if needed.

- **Transparency**

Users are entitled to know who owns and uses their data. Organizations should make it clear what they are gathering and how they plan to use it at the time of data collection. Organizations should notify users of important data processing information after data collection, such as any modifications to the data's use and whomever else it is shared with.

Organizations ought to keep current internal inventories of all the data they possess. Type, degree of sensitivity, compliance requirements, and other pertinent variables should all be taken into consideration when classifying data. Based on these classifications, usage guidelines and access control should be implemented.

- **Consent**

Whenever possible, organizations should obtain user consent before storing, collecting, data processing or sharing. An organization must have a strong justification for retaining or using personal data without the subject's consent, such as using the data to further a common goal or a legal requirement.

A way for data subjects to voice concerns about how their information is managed, or the ability to object must be made available. They should be able to withdraw their permission.

- **Quality**

Organizations ought to aim at ensuring that the information that they gather and store is true. Errors may result in infringements of privacy. As an illustration, when a firm is using an old address in its books, there is the risk of sending private documents to the incorrect individual.

- **Collection, retention and use limitation**

Any data that an Organizational meeting ought to have a specific goal. This objective should be communicated to users, and the data should only be utilized for this purpose. Only the bare minimum of information required for the organization's declared goal should be gathered, and the data should only be retained until that goal is achieved.

- **Design-based privacy**

Privacy should be the default setting for every technology and process used by the organization. Customer privacy should be the company's top priority while developing or deploying any product. Data collection and processing should be discretionary rather than mandatory. It is advised that the user always retain control over their data.

- **Security**

Companies are supposed to adopt mechanisms and procedures to guarantee that user data integrity and confidentiality are maintained.

Businesses can take steps at the process level, like educating employees about their compliance responsibilities and only working with vendors and service providers who respect user privacy.

Organizations can employ a number of methods at the technical controls level to safeguard data. Role-based access control is a policy that Systems for "identity and access management" (IAM) can be used to limit sensitive data access to authorized users only. "Multi-factor authentication" (MFA) and "single sign-on" (SSO) are examples of precise verification procedures that can stop hackers from taking control of genuine users' accounts.

"Data loss prevention" (DLP) tools can locate and classify data, monitor usage, and prevent improper data alteration, sharing, or erasure. Organizations can recover lost or damaged data with the use of data backup and archiving systems.

Data security tools created especially for regulatory compliance can also be used by organizations. These tools frequently have capabilities like audit trails that monitor all pertinent data activity, encryption, and automated policy enforcement.

5.2.4 The 4 Pillars of a Data Governance Framework

An efficient paradigm for data governance is built on four interdependent pillars. Together, they address both the human and technical dimensions of sound data management practices:

- **People:** A governance program is only as strong as the people who run it. This includes data stewards who oversee daily operations, and data owners who are responsible for particular data domains data stewardship responsibilities, data architects who design the structures that support consistent data definitions and data integration, and a data governance committee or data governance council that sets policy and resolves disputes.

The definition of roles will remove ambiguity, will not allow the formation of data silos and will provide accountability that will be distributed properly throughout the organization.

- **Policies:** Data governance strategies are the policies that determine the manner data is developed, stored, used and protected during its data lifecycle.

This consists of the data classification schemes defining sensitive data, access controls defining who is authorized to see or edit particular data objects, and the compliance requirements based on the regulations, including GDPR, CCPA, or HIPAA.

Policies that are well documented act as a single point of truth on how the data can and should be handled and minimizes the risk and earns stakeholder trust.

- **Processes:** Policies need processes that can be repeated effectively. The key data governance processes are metadata management, data quality, data access and entitlements auditing, and the capability to track the data source's ancestry back to its consumption.

These protocols make data governance an ongoing activity integrated into daily data management operations rather than a one-time initiative one that can continue to expand as the volumes of data, source of data and the complexity of the business increases.

- **Technology:** The appropriate technology implements the structure on a large scale. They include discovery and metadata management data catalogs, enabling end-to-end visibility of data flow data lineage tools, maintaining data consistency between business units master data management systems, and holistic governance platforms that impose access controls consistently on all data assets and clouds.

Technology changes governance into an automated auditable feature as opposed to a manual and document-driven undertaking.

5.3 Multi-Cloud and Hybrid Data Architectures

The approaches that companies use multi-cloud and hybrid data structures are used to split workloads and data among many cloud environments or integrate cloud infrastructure with on-premises systems. A multi-cloud strategy makes use of services from several suppliers, like Microsoft Azure, Google Cloud, and Amazon Web Services, to lessen dependency on a single vendor. Conversely, hybrid architecture helps organizations by combining public cloud services with local infrastructure retain control over sensitive information and gain the advantages of cloud scale at the same time.

The main motivation behind the adoption of these architectures is to increase the flexibility, resilience, and performance. Through distributed workloads in several environments, organizations can optimally allocate the resources and choose the most appropriate platform to manage a given task. Fault tolerance is also enhanced by this strategy because failure of the system in one environment can be relieved by relocating operations to a different environment. Consequently, the multi-cloud strategy and the hybrid approach facilitate business continuity and lessen the risk of vendor lock-in.

The other major benefit is regulatory and data governance requirements. Companies with varying geographical locations are usually subjected to diverse legal requirements in terms of information warehouse and processing. Hybrid and multi-cloud solutions also provide the possibility of localizing data, so that the sensitive data can be stored in certain jurisdictions, and the workloads that are not the most important are processed in the cloud. This is a flexibility that assists organizations to comply and still to utilize the advanced cloud capabilities.

Nevertheless, adding these architectures comes at a cost in terms of management, integration, and security. It takes advanced tools and skills to ensure that there are uniform performance, data alignment, and single governance across the various environments. Nevertheless, these challenges do not mean that multi-cloud and hybrid data architectures are no longer a necessity in the contemporary data strategy as organizations seek to strike a balance between control, scalability, and innovativeness in an increasingly distributed digital environment.

5.3.1 Value and Benefits of Multicloud

The main benefit of multicloud for a company is that it avoids vendor lock-in, performance issues, restricted options, or needless expenses that arise from utilizing a single cloud provider. A multicloud approach provides businesses with:

- The flexibility to choose cloud services from several providers based on variables like price and performance, security and compliance needs, and the optimal location for the company.
- The capacity to quickly embrace industry-leading technologies from any vendor as needed or as they become available, as opposed to restricting clients to the products or services that a single vendor provides over time
- Less susceptibility to unplanned downtime and outages because services from other clouds won't always be affected by an outage on one cloud.

- Less vulnerability to security, compatibility, licensing, and other problems brought on by shadow IT users enrolling in cloud services that a single-cloud company might not provide.

5.3.2 Multi-Cloud Architecture: Choosing a Platform

The three primary systems now on "Amazon Web Services" (AWS), Microsoft Azure, and, more recently, "Google Cloud Platform" (GCP) comprise the market. While AWS and Azure are positioned more as general-purpose server/data providers, Google positions itself as the best for AI and machine learning (e.g., image recognition). In a moment, we'll discuss the advantages of utilizing many possibilities simultaneously, but first, let's examine what makes them unique.

- **Amazon Web Services (AWS)**

Because of its strong, well-integrated, and thoroughly tested array of services—which includes networking capabilities, storage options, and processing power—that can handle almost any workload, AWS has long dominated the market. Additionally, it boasts one of the biggest data center networks, offering clients exceptional performance and low latency worldwide. Additionally, AWS provides robust security technologies that are updated on a regular basis to monitor new threats.

- **Microsoft Azure**

Azure's seamless integration Businesses like it because it works well with other Microsoft products and services, including as SQL Server, Windows Server, and Active Directory. Azure's success is hardly surprising considering that Microsoft 365 is used by more than a million businesses globally. In fact, Azure is the largest market share leader when Office 365 is considered when calculating cloud market share. However, once Office 365 is taken out of the picture, AWS reaffirms its dominance in the market. Furthermore, Azure provides its customers with specific support for hybrid cloud deployments, allowing them to easily combine cloud services with on-premises infrastructure.

- **Google Cloud Platform**

Google has lately surpassed the other cloud providers because of its big data and analytics capabilities, which take advantage of its capacity to effectively handle massive datasets and intricate queries. Modern AI and machine learning technologies, like as TensorFlow and AutoML, are drawing in more clients, particularly in view of GCP's reasonable costs and unique offers. Google has made significant contributions to open-source (like Kubernetes) and user-friendly integration for businesses utilizing its business services (such as Gmail for Business, Spreadsheets, Forms, and Google Docs). The fact that more businesses are including GCP into their multicloud infrastructure is therefore not shocking.

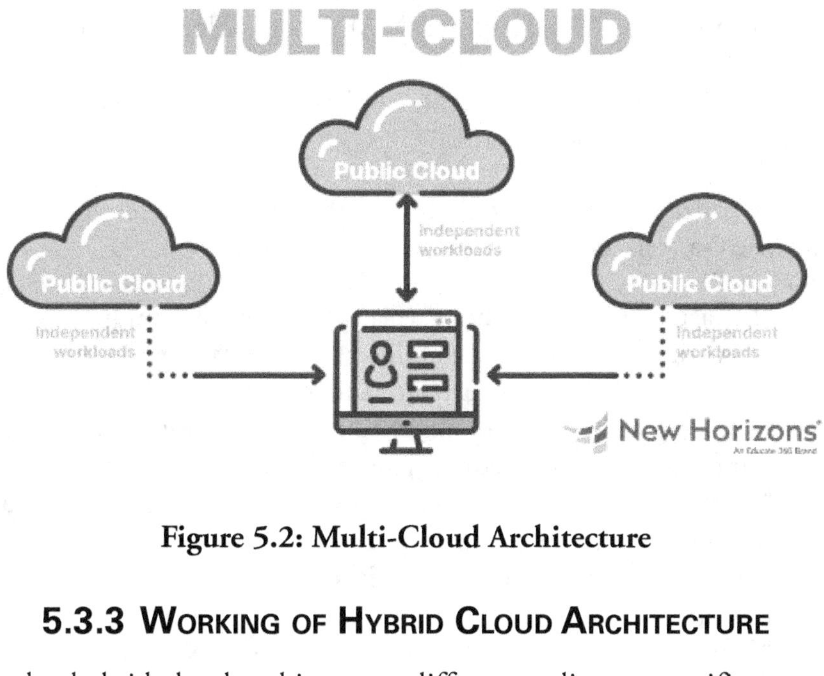

Figure 5.2: Multi-Cloud Architecture

5.3.3 Working of Hybrid Cloud Architecture

Complex hybrid cloud architectures differ according to specific use cases and business requirements. Although there is no one-size-fits-all method for creating hybrid cloud infrastructures, they share a variety of on- and off-premises computing environments, such as the following.

1. Environments that are "on-premises"

Traditional computing involves a company employing hardware and servers at its own physical location, like an office building or an on-premises data center, to govern and manage networking, storage, software, and computer resources.

2. Cloud environments that are private

a cloud computing environment in which every resource is separate and used exclusively by one company. Many of the advantages of cloud computing are combined with the security and management of on-premises IT infrastructure in a private cloud.

3. Cloud environments that are public

cloud computing that is housed by a third-party cloud service provider (CSP), such Amazon Web Services (AWS), Google Cloud, Microsoft Azure, or IBM Cloud. These public cloud service providers use the public internet to host individual virtual machines (VM) and other cloud computing services on a pay-per-use basis.

The majority of large firms use all three of the above cloud provider services, while many midsized businesses use more than one:

- "Infrastructure-as-a-Service" (IaaS) offers pay-as-you-go computing, network, and storage capabilities to clients via the internet. By enabling end users to expand and contract resources as needed, IaaS lessens the need for significant upfront capital investments or unnecessary "owned" equipment, especially during demand spikes.
- "Platform-as-a-Service" (PaaS) provides a complete cloud platform (hardware, software, and infrastructure) for developing, running, and managing applications without the cost, complexity, and rigidity of building and maintaining that platform on-site.
- "Software-as-a-Service" (SaaS) is the term used to describe cloud-hosted application software for end-user applications, such as Dropbox and Zoom. The SaaS service provider is responsible for operating, managing, and maintaining the software and its supporting infrastructure. SaaS is the most widely used paradigm for software delivery and the most widely used public cloud service.

5.3.4 Benefits of Multi-Cloud Architecture

1. Cost Optimization and Flexibility

Businesses are constantly searching for methods to streamline processes and save costs. Accepting a multi-cloud approach is an excellent option that can offer numerous operational and financial benefits. In addition to offering organizations a degree of freedom that they cannot have by working with a single vendor, this strategy can help them save a substantial amount of money. You should concentrate on the following when designing a multi-cloud:

- **Preventing vendor lock-in:** By utilizing several platforms, businesses are free from the cost and service restrictions of a single vendor. When faced with possible price increases, they can swap vendors and select the most economical alternative for particular workloads. Flexibility in business equates to agility, and with the elimination of data egress fees, businesses may now embrace a multicloud approach and shift workloads as required for cost optimization, features, etc.
- **Aligning price with resource requirements:** Various cloud providers have different pricing structures and focus on different kinds of resources. By utilizing many options, you can maximize your spending by utilizing the most economical choice for every kind of task and service.
- **Taking advantage of regional pricing:** Businesses that can split their workloads among the most economical locations stand to benefit from a multicloud strategy because providers frequently provide reduced prices in particular regions.

2. Improved Performance and Reliability

Businesses are better positioned to reduce downtime, improve service delivery to users worldwide, and access cutting-edge technology customized to meet their specific requirements when they implement a multi-cloud strategy. The following advantages in terms of performance and dependability are to be expected:

- **Fewer outages:** The spread of workloads to work on many platforms implies that businesses can reduce the possibility of errors or interruptions in a single cloud.
- **Geographic distribution of latency-sensitive applications:** In order to accommodate low-latency applications or geographically dispersed consumers, a multiload deployment can be used to place applications in the regions that are nearest to the final users, which enhances performance and user experience.

The different providers have advantages in different fields, so the smart companies structure their strategy to access the best services of each provider.

3. Enhanced Security and Compliance

Businesses can establish a framework that enhances security and guarantees compliance with all applicable rules by implementing a multi-cloud architecture. Businesses may By sharing information, they may disperse their risk and build additional safety nets and apps over many cloud platforms.

- **Better data security posture:** By dispersing data throughout several clouds, attackers may find it more difficult to target a single point of entry. Furthermore, a multicloud solution might assist comply with legislation that may require data residency in particular areas.
- **Business continuity and catastrophe recovery:** Better alternatives for disaster recovery are ensured by replicating important data and apps across several clouds. In the event that one is disrupted, the others can go on, reducing downtime and data loss.
- **Fulfilling a variety of compliance standards:** Businesses operating in various industries or geographical areas may be subject to different rules, and various suppliers can assist them in fulfilling the particular compliance requirements for each assignment.

4. Innovation and Agility

The ability to utilize various cloud providers provides the companies with a wider variety of the technologies and functionalities. This does not only increase their choices, but it also accelerates the development process enabling them to roll out and launch products quicker. Organizations may also anticipate:

- **Access to a wider range of services and features:** By using many cloud providers, businesses can develop and implement applications that would not be feasible with a single provider.
- **Shorter time-to-market:** Choosing the best cloud service for a given need helps expedite development and deployment and shorten the time needed to bring goods and services to market.

- **Testing new technologies:** Major corporations' innovative offerings can enable customers to test and be above the curve of innovation.

One should also keep in mind that this is not a universal solution but only companies need to evaluate their goals, needs, and resources prior to putting a multiload strategy into practice. The difficulty in controlling several cloud environments must be compared with the possible advantages to see the successful implementation.

5.3.5 Benefits of Hybrid Cloud Architecture

The following are some of the many benefits of a hybrid cloud architecture:

1. Agility and scalability

By quickly allocating and releasing resources stored on-site or in public or private clouds, hybrid cloud architecture increases agility and makes it simple to adapt to changing business needs. Because hybrid clouds use on-demand cloud resources, they also provide nearly infinite scalability up or down.

2. Business continuity

By replicating mission-critical data to the cloud and enabling scaling during demand spikes, hybrid cloud deployment maximizes business continuity and reduces downtime.

3. Cost savings

By moving workloads to the public cloud and avoiding the continuous expenses associated with maintaining and replacing outdated hardware, a hybrid cloud strategy can assist reduce capital costs.

4. Modernization application

The flexibility and security offered by a hybrid cloud environment enable the process of "application modernization," which is the conversion of legacy software to scalable, cloud-native app environments. This makes it possible to design apps quickly, deploy them automatically, and update them frequently, so eliminating waterfall development methods.

5. Generative AI adoption

By offering limitless storage space, computing power, and quick scalability, hybrid cloud architecture speeds up generative AI and its heavy reliance on massive volumes of data and "large language models" (LLMs).

5.3.6 Challenges of Multi-Cloud Architecture

Re-platforming your IT infrastructure is part of the multicloud journey, which affects everyone from networking teams and IT operators to developers and security teams.

Despite the clear advantages, managing several services and suppliers' makes IT governance more difficult and calls for complex coordination and management techniques. Additionally, as data transfers from one cloud to another with possibly different security protocols and compliance standards, data security and regulatory compliance become more difficult in a multicloud scenario.

It's critical to comprehend the difficulties associated with adopting a multicloud strategy so that you can create or contract out the required training for your staff.

- **Skills Gaps and Knowledge Deficits**

Since new hires might not be familiar with multicloud principles or particular platforms, training should start as soon as they join the team. Additionally, new features, services, and best practices are being offered daily due to the cloud environment's quick and continual evolution. As a result, current IT staff may need to improve their competences and be able to achieve incomes across several schemes.

- **Performance and Management Concerns.**

It is difficult to provide, monitor, and regulate resources when there are multiple platforms. Keeping an eye on It can be difficult to manage costs across several clouds, particularly when different service providers alter their rates at different periods. Software and data security issues in different cloud environments should be taken into consideration, and businesses must ensure that they have a strong plan and are familiar with security best practices.

- **Interoperability and Integration Problems.**

There may be a possible inconsistency and compatibility problem when integrating data and applications across various platforms. In the development of a multicloud architecture, IT should ensure that the individual clouds and their services are compatible with each other, which requires sophisticated integration tools to keep the platform-to-platform operations seamless.

5.3.7 Best Practices in Multi-Cloud Architecture Implementation.

Although multi-cloud architecture is a sophisticated solution, it offers resilience, scalability, and flexibility. To maximize operations, security, performance, and cost-efficiency, organizations require a strategic strategy. Because of this, it's critical to become proficient in these best practices:

- **Comprehensive Planning**

This strategy can assist you in achieving your company's objectives, so start with a clear grasp of them. Make a detailed plan that includes determining the best providers for certain jobs, evaluating your present and future needs, and establishing specific goals for each cloud environment.

- **Compliance and Data Governance**

To guarantee that data is appropriately managed across all platforms, establish strong data governance principles. This includes adhering to rules unique to your sector and the areas where you conduct business. Your multicloud deployment approach should take data sovereignty, privacy legislation, and regulatory obligations into careful consideration.

- **Budget Efficiency**

Use cost management techniques and tools to keep an eye on and limit expenditures. If you have several vendors, it can be difficult to keep track of subscriptions, which can have an adverse effect on your budget. This entails Although multi-cloud architecture is a sophisticated solution, it offers resilience, scalability, and flexibility. To maximize operations, security, performance, and cost-efficiency, organizations require a strategic strategy. Because of this, it's critical to become proficient in these best practices:

- **Security Strategy**

Establish an overall cloud security policy. Although this is not a solution to data and application security, to prevent the occurrence of security breaches and vulnerabilities, implement a similar security policy, including threat monitoring systems, encryption techniques, and identity and access controls in a variety of settings.

- **Automation and DevOps Practices.**

Utilize DevOps standards and automation tools to streamline procedures and improve cloud infrastructure efficiency. Automation of the Processes for deployment, scaling, and management lower the possibility of human error and manages to allocate precious resources to more strategic activities.

- **Proficiency training and group training.**

Make sure that you have the skills in your team to handle multicloud environments. This is through constant training and development of systems to be on schedule with the evolving best practices and cloud technology. Consider alternative cloud platforms' certifications and specialized training that address the following areas:

  - Making judgements based on information about features, cost, security, and compliance.
  - The ability to assess business needs, build architecture, and create effective multicloud strategies.
  - Training to become independent of the platform's functions and become cloud-agnostic.
  - Offering methods for smooth application integration and data transfer
  - Filling in knowledge gaps and keeping up with the most recent developments in multicloud technology.
  - Giving workers the freedom to take up new tasks and adjust to evolving processes.
  - Techniques for allocating resources, optimizing costs, and determining the most economical alternatives to particular loads.
  - Learning and applying security best practices unique to multiclouds deployments.

Choose and use the tools that can be involved to integrate and handle numerous cloud environments. Find management systems that provide platform visibility on performance, affordability, and security to enable prompt decision-making and modification.

- **Portability and interoperability.**

Adopt standards and technologies, such as containers and microservices, that enable data and applications to be transferred between different cloud environments designs to be in a position to circumvent lock-in with vendors and can transfer with ease to dissimilar clouds.

- **Regular Evaluation and Adjustments**

Make sure your strategy is in line with evolving business requirements and technical developments by reviewing and evaluating it on a regular basis. To maximize performance and minimize expenses, be ready to modify your strategy and move resources between clouds as necessary.

5.4 AI and Machine Learning Integration with Data Systems

The concept of incorporating "Artificial Intelligence" (AI) and "Machine Learning" (ML) into the data systems can be defined as the process of integrating intelligent algorithms into data frameworks to allow automated information analysis, future prediction, and decision-making. Data systems of traditional nature are mainly concerned with the storage and retrieval of information but the AI-enabled ones are more advanced since they can learn patterns of data and produce insights. As a result of the technologies connected to Artificial Intelligence and to Machine Learning, systems can be used to process a vast amount of structured and unstructured information in an efficient way.

The interaction between AI and ML helps to improve the functionality of modern data platforms and allows running high-quality analytics, including predictive models, anomaly detection, and recommendation systems. Organizations do not have to confine themselves to the use of static queries alone but can use smart models to predict trends, risks and optimize operations. This transition takes data systems out of their passive repositories to active and decision support tools that integrate constantly via the help of the learning process.

A data pipeline, which can be applied to train and deploy models, is an important aspect of this integration. Prior to the utilization of data to train machine learning models, data must be first collected, cleaned, and transformed. These models are then implemented in data systems as they produce real-time or batch predictions. Automated workflows are frequently used in platforms to service such a lifecycle to guarantee the accuracy and applicability of models as new data becomes available.

Although it has its benefits, the implementation of AI and ML combined with data systems has several difficulties such as the problem of data quality, interpretability of models, and computation. Ethical use of data and transparency in automated decision-making are also significant aspects that should be considered. However, the introduction of intelligent technologies keeps on redefining how organizations derive value out of data thus it will remain a major element of contemporary data architectures.

5.4.1 Understanding of AI Data Management

AI data management is the application of "artificial intelligence" (AI) and "machine learning" (ML) to the data management lifecycle. Examples include using AI to speed up or automate data collection, cleaning, analysis, security, and other data management processes.

Data management can benefit from both more sophisticated generative AI models and conventional, rules-based AI.

Modern firms control enormous volumes of information on anything from personnel records and customer preferences to financial transactions and product stocks. Businesses can outperform their rivals by using this data to guide organisational activities and decision-making.

However, it is difficult to guarantee that these massive datasets are reliable, accurate, and adequately accessible for real-world usage.

By streamlining processes like merging data sources, cleansing data, and retrieving data, AI and ML solutions can assist organisations in making the most of their data. Businesses are able to make more data-driven choices as a result.

Additionally, AI data management assists businesses in creating the superior data pipelines needed to develop and execute their own machine learning algorithms and AI models.

5.4.2 Necessity to Prepare Data for Machine Learning

The process of organizing, cleaning, and transforming raw data so that AI and machine learning models can analyses it efficiently is known as data preparation.

In data science and machine learning initiatives, preprocessing data is an essential first step. It improves machine learning model performance and allows companies to extract useful insights from their data.

The capacity to enhance raw datasets and expedite the model training process makes data preparation crucial to AI and machine learning. You may make more accurate forecasts, find new relationships in the data, and produce insightful information that will help you make better decisions by correctly preparing the data.

Here are some basic methods for efficiently preparing data:

- **Converting unstructured or semi-structured** data into a structured format makes it easier for algorithms to process the information.
- **Finding and handling missing values:** To avoid distorting the analysis, missing values should be filled in or records with incomplete information should be eliminated.
- **Eliminating duplicate or inaccurate entries:** By removing mistakes that may otherwise compromise model correctness, this phase helps preserve the integrity of your dataset.
- **Normalisation and scaling:** By standardising feature scales, biases in models can be minimised by accurately accounting for differences across features.

Clean, relevant, and properly formatted data enables machine learning models to learn from given inputs and make accurate predictions efficiently.

5.4.3 AI data management Benefits

By automating laborious processes like data finding, cleaning, and cataloguing and simplifying data retrieval and analysis, artificial intelligence (AI) has the potential to revolutionize data management. Businesses may create more effective data management procedures that are less error-prone and more supportive of data science, AI projects, and data privacy.

- **Realizing the full value of big data for business**

According to AvePoint's AI and Information Management Report, at least one petabyte of data was managed by 64% of the organizations polled.1 To put things into perspective, that amounts to about nine quadrillion bits of data. Additionally, a large portion of it is in unstructured formats like text files, pictures, and videos.

Data scientists can benefit much from all of this information, but handling such complicated data in such large amounts by hand is not feasible. By automating crucial processes like discovery, integration, and cleansing, AI and ML solutions can make this data accessible.

Organizations can employ clean and easily accessible data for sophisticated data analytics initiatives, such as a predictive analytics project that forecasts future trends in consumer purchasing based on existing data.

AI technology can potentially improve data accessibility for non-data scientists. More users across the company may use data to guide their decisions thanks to user-friendly data catalogues with automated visualizations and database interfaces driven by LLM.

- **Fueling AI initiatives**

59% of CEOs think that having the most cutting-edge generative AI will be essential to an organization's future competitive advantage. Organizations require consistent sources of high-quality, clean data in order to develop and use those AI models.

AI tools facilitate the development of reliable, the data pipelines that businesses need in order to train their own AI and ML models by simplifying data administration. Additionally, these models can be educated to carry out duties and resolve issues unique to the company and its clients because they can be trained on the company's data.

- **USING DATA WHILE REMAINING COMPLIANT**

AI-enabled security and governance systems assist in preventing costly cyberattacks and data breaches. Additionally, they enable businesses to use their data while adhering to data privacy and protection laws such as the Payment Card Industry Data Security Standard (PCI-DSS) and GDPR.

By automatically implementing suitable safeguards and data use guidelines, AI-enabled data management can be beneficial. In this manner, the data is only accessible to authorized individuals, who may only utilize it in accordance with business policy and industry requirements.

Additionally, Synthetic data generators can help by creating datasets that faithfully capture broad patterns while removing private information that might not be allowed to be utilized in certain contexts by an organization.

5.4.4 AI DATA MANAGEMENT USE CASES

While AI and ML can be applied to nearly every facet of the data management process, the following are some of the most common uses:

- Locating information
- Data quality
- Data accessibility
- Data security

1. DATA DISCOVERY

Businesses today deal with a lot of data from a wide range of sources and in a number of formats. This data is managed by multiple users and eventually distributed over public and private clouds, on-premises storage systems, and even the individual endpoints of employees.

Two issues are raised by the difficulty of centrally tracking and managing all of this data.

First, if an organization is unaware that a dataset exists, it cannot use it.

Second, there are security dangers associated with this unmanaged and unknown "shadow data." Shadow data is involved in one-third of data breaches. These breaches cost USD 5.27 million on average, which is 16% more than the average cost of all breaches.

Businesses may have more control and visibility over all of their data assets by using AI and ML to automate many aspects of data discovery.

Applications of AI in data discovery include:

- Data storage repositories and network devices can be automatically scanned by AI-powered data discovery tools, which can index fresh data very instantly.
- New data can be tagged by automated data classification techniques using machine learning models or pre-established criteria. For instance, any nine-digit number in the XXX-XX-XXXX format might be recognised by the application as a US social security number.
- Structured data can be extracted from unstructured data sources using LLMs and other natural language processing methods. For example, job seekers' contact information and experience can be extracted from text-document resumes in a variety of forms.

2. Data Accessibility

Many organisations are unable to fully utilise their data because of data silos. By substituting unified data fabrics for segregated repositories, AI and ML can expedite data integration initiatives. The necessary data assets are available to users throughout the company at any time.

AI applications in Data access consists of:

- Data integration tools powered by AI enable the company to integrate or merge various datasets by automatically identifying their relationships.
- By producing AI-capable metadata management platforms can describe data assets using tagging and classification assist in automating the construction of data catalogues.
- Natural language instructions can be accepted and processed

by databases and data catalogues with LLM-powered interfaces, enabling users to locate data assets and products without the need for SQL queries or special code. Additionally, some LLM-powered interfaces can assist users in improving datasets, refining queries, or recommending relevant datapoints.

- By examining workload trends and streamlining query execution, Machine learning methods can be used by AI-enabled query engines to improve database efficiency.

3. Data security

Data security should be given top priority because there is a business reason for it. An average data breach costs an organization USD 4.88 million in lost revenue, system downtime, reputational damage, and response costs, according to the Cost of a Data Breach report.

Security policy enforcement, breach detection, and unauthorised activity blocking are all made possible by AI and ML. AI applications in data safety comprise:

- Sensitive data, including "personally identifiable information" (PII), can be automatically identified by AI-driven data loss protection systems applying security measures, and flagging or preventing unauthorised usage of that data.
- AI and ML algorithms are used by anomaly-based threat detection systems like "endpoint detection and response" (EDR) and "user and entity behaviour analytics" (UEBA) to track network activity. They identify questionable departures from the norm, like a large amount of data abruptly shifting to a new place.
- Organisations can use LLMs to develop and implement data governance policies. For example, in a "role-based access control" (RBAC) system, an LLM can help the security team define the different roles and corresponding permissions. It is also possible to convert these role definitions into identity and access management system rules with the assistance of the LLM.
- AI-enabled fraud detection technologies can identify anomalous transactions by analysing trends using AI and ML.

5.4.5 Challenges in Data Integration for Machine Learning

The process of machine learning projects data integration can offer multiple challenges, which may have an impact on efficiency and desired results. The following are some of the common challenges that are encountered in the process of data integration:

- **Incompatible and formatting:** Multiple source datasets may be of different formats, schemas, and structures and have to be significantly standardized and adjusted to be compatible with machine learning models.
- **Security and privacy issues:** In the case of sensitive data, it's crucial to ensure that very high levels of security measures are enforced to prevent unauthorized access or breaching and comply with the regulations.
- **Data volume, velocity, and variety:** Because of the sheer volume of data, the various forms it can take (structured, semi-structured, or unstructured), and the rapid rate at which data is being streamed, integrating big data can be a challenging task may require processing.
- **Integration of legacy systems:** Integration of outdated systems into new platforms for data consolidation may be severely hampered by their lack of API access or contemporary integration capabilities.

By utilizing a well-integrated dataset that increases the model's accuracy and efficiency, overcoming these obstacles improves machine learning performance.

5.4.6 Next-Generation Data Platform Innovations

It's crucial to recognize the effects of legacy technology, but you also need to know what alternatives are available. There are distinct definitions for the phrases "data," "data management," and "data platform." According to this definition, a next-generation data platform is one that supports flexible and versatile data models, provides a variety of access patterns (such as document, relational, and graph), and meets the needs of small and large organizations for new development or modernization initiatives in terms of speed, scale, performance, integration, and security. All of this is contained in a single platform that supports a business by providing reliable, consistent, and real-time data. It is a fact that safe data must be delivered "end-to-end" from a mobile device to an embedded device (imagine an electric vehicle), and then to the data in the back-office systems and analytical functions.

Nearly 90% of the global IT and data platform decision-makers in the fintech and financial services industries surveyed claim to already use a next-generation data platform. Additionally, nearly three quarters (74%) of respondents are aware that a next-generation data platform will enable faster software builds and iterating at scale (76%), freeing up team members to concentrate on creativity in addition to the benefits of technology.

5.4.7 Key Lessons from Real-World Implementations

1. Design for Scalability from Day One

One of the most critical aspects of building a data platform is scalability. The performance should remain unchanged as the volume of data is growing exponentially and the platform can readily fulfill the requirements. To achieve scalability, one needs:

- **Distributed Computing:** Use solutions such as Apache Spark and Hadoop to process data in many nodes.
- **Cloud-Native Architecture:** Elastic scalability and resource optimization: Use platforms such as AWS, Azure, or Google cloud.
- **Containerization:** Containerized applications are deployed with Kubernetes to provide consistency and adaptability based on environment.

2. Embrace a Data Mesh Approach

A big data system can easily be reduced to bottlenecks. A data mesh architecture decentralizes data ownership and delegates the responsibility to domain teams. This method creates teamwork, minimizes redundancy and increases the speed of access to data.

3. Automate Everything

Efficiency in modern data platforms is anchored on automation. Automation of repetitive tasks increases the speed and alleviates errors between data ingestion and deployment pipelines as well. Key areas to focus on include:

- **Data Ingestion Pipelines:** Manage real-time and batch data ingestion using systems such as Apache Kafka or AWS Glue.
- **CI/CD Pipelines:** Manualize deployments with Jenkins, GitLab CI/CD, or Azure Devops.
- **Data Quality Checks:** Automated checks should be used to check whether the data is accurate and consistent.

4. Prioritize Governance and Security

As more laws regarding data privacy are being introduced, governance and security are not negotiable. A powerful platform should consist of:

- **Data Lineage and Cataloging:** In order to monitor data provenance and ensure transparency, use such tools as Alation or Apache Atlas.
- **Access Control:** Have role-based access control (RBAC) and encryption to protect sensitive data.
- **Compliance:** Make certain to meet such regulations as GDPR, HIPAA, and CCPA.

5. Develop Self-Service Analytics.

Agility can be greatly enhanced by empowering the business people through the capacity to obtain and examine data without the involvement of IT. The process of creating an intuitive self-service system requires:

- **Data Virtualization:** Virtualize different sources of data with tools such as Trino or Starburst.
- **User-Friendly Interfaces:** Design dashboards and visualization tools in a simple way.
- **Metadata Management:** Help users to learn about and learn about datasets with ease.

5.4.8 Impact of Next-Generation Data Intelligence Platforms on Business Operations

The skill of making decisions and utilizing the resources effectively has become more important in the contemporary business world, which is highly competitive. Nevertheless, a significant number of companies are still struggling with data silos and the intricate nature of integrating the different technologies employed in managing and analytics of data. These constraints usually limit the good use of data in business functions. Data intelligence systems solve these issues because they allow organizations to leave the old methods of data processing behind and provide insights relevant to the specific user roles and workflows.

Next-generation data intelligence systems offer a common framework, which incorporates data along with analytics and intelligent technology into a single system. These solutions are meant to convert raw data into valuable insights that can be used to make both strategic and operational decisions. They increase efficiency and promptness of the entire organization by aligning data with the business goals and needs of the users.

This is why such platforms become a game changer:

- **THE DATA INTEGRATION AND MANAGEMENT WILL BE IMPROVED:**

The next-generation data intelligence systems combine the data of various sources, such as structured and unstructured information (IoT systems, social media, and external databases). This integration helps firms to come up with an extensive knowledge of their operations. The platforms, by creating connections between data and business processes, offer an overall perspective of important entities (customers, products, suppliers, and employees), which is why they facilitate quicker and better-informed decision-making.

- **THE USE OF PREDICTIVE AND PRESCRIPTIVE AI/ML MODELS:**

These platforms are based on the skills of the Artificial Intelligence and the Machine Learning to offer predictive and prescriptive insights. Predictive models help organizations to foresee trends, customer behavior, and other possible disruptions whereas prescriptive models suggest the right course of action to maximize results. Such proactive attitude increases productivity and helps to minimize expenses.

Certainly, the company has enhanced decision-making abilities regarding its creative processes and products.

- **ENHANCED DECISION-MAKING POWERS:**

Decision-makers will have the opportunity to use real-time data and powerful analytic tools, which will ensure the availability of precise and updated information. Data abstraction and visualization tools make complex sets of data even easier and allow the stakeholders to process the insights and make the proper course of action timely.

The company is able to conduct its business processes adhering to a specific method in order to enhance its efficiency and automatize the processes as well.

- **Automation and Operational efficiency:**

The use of data intelligence platforms assists in automating routine processes which results in less manual intervention and low chances of human error. These platforms are beneficial in the sense that they facilitate better resource use and high performance of operations by simplifying workflows and delivering actionable insights to guide operations.

- o **Scalability:** The servers are capable of being scaled to support the full performance of the new system. The servers can be scaled to accommodate the entire performance of the new system.

These systems are scaled to match the growth of the organization and the changing business needs. They welcome various deployment models such as cloud, on-premises and hybrid environments wherein, they are adaptable to different contexts of operation and technological infrastructure.

- **Enhanced User Experience:**

These platforms enhance usability and user satisfaction by providing custom interfaces and role-based access to insights. The accessibility in the form of clouds also allows users to get data and insights no matter where they are, allowing to collaborate and make informed decisions throughout the organization.

Numerous technology vendors, such as Microsoft, Oracle, and Google, have all-encompassing data intelligence platforms which are a combination of data integration, analytics, and AI-driven features. To illustrate, Oracle Fusion Data Intelligence Platform provides data-as-a-service, which is an automated pipeline, built-in data models, sophisticated analytics, and smart applications that help organizations to deliver better business results.

5.4.9 Future Trends in Next-Generation Data Platform Innovations

As requirements on the complexity and the needs of the data grow, next-generation data platforms are bound to evolve rapidly as more organizations adopt the new sophisticated data technologies. There is the trend of more intelligent, automated and decentralized data ecosystems, according to emerging trends. These platforms are continuously introducing additional capabilities of Artificial Intelligence and Machine Learning to enable self-optimizing data pipelines, automated data quality control, and more powerful predictive analytics.

The other significant trend is the growing utilization of multi-cloud as well as hybrid data architecture in which organizations can distribute workloads across the different settings to achieve greater flexibility and resiliency. The strategy aids in reducing dependence on a single supplier and enables regulatory requirements of data localization. Also, the emergence of data fabric and data mesh frameworks is changing the ways of accessing and managing data, which facilitates decentralized ownership and enhanced access to data within organizations.

The next generation platforms are also starting to be characterized by real time data processing. Companies are becoming more in need of real-time information that enables them to react to unstable business environments, changing customer patterns, and fluctuations in operations. Consequently, data platforms are being augmented with streaming data technologies and event driven architectures to enable them to support continuous data processing and instant decision-making abilities.

Moreover, data governance, security, as well as ethical data usage is increasingly emphasized upon. As more regulations come under closer inspection and the issue of data privacy is brought up, companies are putting together more effective governance structures to promote compliance and transparency. It is assumed that the future data platforms will include inherent governance, privacy-enhancing practices, and responsible AI application, allowing organizations to be innovative without breaching trust and accountability.

Multiple Choice Questions (MCQs)

1. **What is a key advantage of serverless data platforms?**
   A. They require manual infrastructure scaling
   B. They eliminate the need for internet access
   C. They automatically scale based on workload demand
   D. They only support on-premises deployment

2. **Which of the following is a major challenge in data governance?**
   A. Reducing cloud storage capacity
   B. Ensuring data quality, security, and compliance
   C. Eliminating all data backups
   D. Increasing hardware dependency

3. **Data privacy regulations such as GDPR and CCPA mainly focus on:**
   A. Increasing server speed
   B. Protecting personal and sensitive user data
   C. Reducing the use of AI in businesses
   D. Expanding database storage size

4. **What is the primary benefit of a multi-cloud data architecture?**
   A. Dependence on a single cloud vendor
   B. Improved flexibility and reduced vendor lock-in
   C. Elimination of all cybersecurity risks
   D. Lower need for data integration tools

5. **Hybrid data architectures combine:**
   A. Public cloud and on-premises infrastructure
   B. Only private cloud systems
   C. Only traditional relational databases
   D. Only edge devices and mobile apps

6. **How does AI integration improve modern data platforms?**
   A. By replacing all human decision-making
   B. By reducing the need for data storage
   C. By enabling predictive analytics and intelligent automation
   D. By eliminating the use of cloud computing

7. **Which machine learning capability is commonly integrated into future data platforms?**
   A. Manual data entry
   B. Automated anomaly detection
   C. Paper-based reporting
   D. Static dashboard design

8. **What is one expected innovation in next-generation data platforms?**
   A. Complete removal of metadata
   B. Increased use of intelligent automation and self-managing systems
   C. Dependence only on local hard drives
   D. Elimination of analytics tools

9. **Why is data governance becoming more important in future data platforms?**
   A. Because organizations are using less data
   B. Because data is becoming more distributed, valuable, and regulated
   C. Because cloud platforms are disappearing
   D. Because databases no longer need security

10. **Which of the following best describes the future of data platforms?**
    A. More isolated systems with less automation
    B. Greater integration of cloud, AI, governance, and scalability
    C. Exclusive use of spreadsheets for analytics
    D. Reduced need for data-driven decision-making

Answers

1	2	3	4	5	6	7	8	9	10
C	B	B	B	A	C	B	B	B	B

References

Ahmed, S. T., Syed, A., & Basha, S. M. (2021). *Big dat a Analyt ics Big Analyt ics* (S. T. Ahmed (ed.)). Milestone Research Publications.

AL-Jumaili, A. H. A., Muniyandi, R. C., Hasan, M. K., Paw, J. K. S., & Singh, M. J. (2023). Big Data Analytics Using Cloud Computing Based Frameworks for Power Management Systems: Status, Constraints, and Future Recommendations. *Sensors, 23*(6), 2952. https://doi.org/10.3390/s23062952

Anomalo. (2024). *Data Ingestion vs Data Integration: Understanding Key Differences.* https://www.anomalo.com/blog/data-ingestion-vs-data-integration-understanding-key-differences/

Assunção, M. D., Calheiros, R. N., Bianchi, S., Netto, M. A. S., & Buyya, R. (2015). Big Data computing and clouds: Trends and future directions. *Journal of Parallel and Distributed Computing, 79–80*, 3–15. https://doi.org/10.1016/j.jpdc.2014.08.003

Dagster. (2026). *Data Engineering Tools: Types, Features, and 10 Essential Tools.* https://dagster.io/guides/data-engineering-tools-types-features-and-10-essential-tools-xsde6

Hwang, K., & Chen, M. (2017). *Big-Data Anaytics - for Cloud, IoT and Cognitive Learning.*

Orr, E. (2026). *15 Data Engineering Best Practices to Follow in 2026.* LakeFS. https://lakefs.io/blog/data-engineering-best-practices/

Verma, V. (2022). Big Data and Cloud Databases Revolutionizing Business Intelligence. *TIJER – International Research Journal, 9*(1), 48–58.

About The Authors

Manoj Kumar is an engineering leader, data architecture expert, and cybersecurity strategist currently shaping secure enterprise systems at Microsoft. With over 20 years spanning software development, big data, and AI/ML security, his career merges scaling massive data infrastructures with protecting them. He has modernized petabyte-scale databases and architected telemetry platforms processing 3.5 PB of daily data. He also architected real-time data pipelines processing over one trillion events daily at petabyte scale. A CISSP and CCISO-certified professional with an M.S. in Cybersecurity, an MBA, and a US patent, Manoj champions intelligent, secure cloud data solutions, blending technical rigor with practical insight to solve real-world challenges.

Purushotham Jinka is a Vice President at Citibank with 16 years of experience building and operating mission-critical data and cloud platforms within highly regulated financial environments. He specializes in service reliability, incident management, automation, and performance engineering across Snowflake, Teradata, and Amazon Web Services ecosystems.

Purushotham has a proven track record of leading reliability initiatives, reducing operational risk, and driving scalable solutions through cross-functional collaboration with application, infrastructure, and cloud teams. He holds an MBA from University of Arizona and is a certified Teradata Solution Architect.

He has authored research papers and actively contributes to the data engineering community through IEEE, ISACA, IOASD, IETE, RAPTORs Fellowship & Sigma Xi. He is passionate about making data warehousing practical, accessible, and less intimidating.

Prakash Parida is a technology leader and Director at CGI with over 18 years of experience in driving enterprise transformation through cloud computing, artificial intelligence, and digital innovation. An AWS Certified Solutions Architect and IEEE Senior Member, he brings deep expertise in designing scalable, intelligent systems that enable organizations to thrive in an increasingly complex digital landscape.

Throughout his career, Prakash has led large-scale initiatives across diverse industries, combining strategic vision with hands-on technical leadership to deliver impactful, real-world solutions. His work focuses on cloud modernization, AI-driven architectures, and building resilient, future-ready enterprises.

A published researcher with multiple papers presented at IEEE conferences, Prakash is passionate about advancing technology at the intersection of industry and academia. He is committed to sharing knowledge, fostering innovation, and helping organizations harness emerging technologies to solve meaningful challenges.

Shyam Goyal is a data analytics professional and business intelligence strategist, currently driving data-driven decision-making at Samsung Electronics America as a Data Analyst III. His career bridges the intersection of technology and business, with deep expertise in solving complex organizational challenges through advanced analytics, machine learning, data engineering, and tools like Python, machine learning, Tableau. He is a vivid learner holding a B. Tech in Computer Science, an MBA, and an MS in Business Analytics from UC Irvine. Currently pursuing a Doctorate in Business Administration. Shyam brings both academic rigor and real-world precision to every problem he tackles, transforming raw data into actionable intelligence for enterprise-scale impact.

www.ingramcontent.com/pod-product-compliance
Lightning Source LLC
LaVergne TN
LVHW022211200926
848481LV00006B/1922
* 9 7 9 8 9 0 4 5 1 1 3 7 1 *